UNIVERSITY OF WAI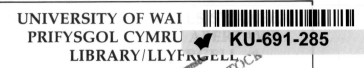
PRIFYSGOL CYMRU
LIBRARY/LLYFRGELL

Classmark   N8354

Location   Minerva Library

1004289007

Women, Art, and Power
and Other Essays

Linda Nochlin

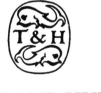

THAMES AND HUDSON

Any copy of this book issued by the publisher as a paperback is
sold subject to the condition that it shall not by way of trade or
otherwise be lent, resold, hired out or otherwise circulated
without the publisher's prior consent in any form of binding or
cover other than that in which it is published and without a
similar condition including these words being imposed on a
subsequent purchaser.

First published in Great Britain in 1989 by
Thames and Hudson Ltd, London

Reprinted 1994

Originally published in the United States in 1988
by Harper & Row, Publishers, Inc.
Copyright © 1988 Linda Nochlin

All Rights Reserved. No part of this publication may be
reproduced or transmitted in any form or by any means,
electronic or mechanical, including photocopy, recording or
any other information storage and retrieval system, without
prior permission in writing from the publisher.

British Library Cataloguing-in-Publication Data
A catalogue record for this book is available from
the British Library
0-500-27577-7

Printed and bound in the USA

UNIVERSITY COLLEGE
LIBRARY
SWANSEA

Contents

———

———

List of Illustrations

1 Women, Art, and Power

1. Jacques-Louis David. *The Oath of the Horatii*. Paris, Louvre
2. Sir Joseph Noel Paton. *In Memoriam*. Engraving after the lost original painting
3. Francisco Goya y Lucientes. *And They Are Like Wild Beasts*. Etching and aquatint
4. *Woman Toppling Policeman with a Jujitsu Throw*. Photograph
5. Eugène Delacroix. *The Death of Sardanapalus*. Paris, Louvre
6. Jean-Léon Gérôme. *Oriental Slave Market*. Williamstown, Clark Collection
7. Édouard Manet. *The Ball at the Opera*. Washington, D.C., National Gallery of Art
8. André Kertesz. *Dancer's Legs*. Photograph
9. Emily Mary Osborn. *Nameless and Friendless*. Collection Sir David Scott
10. Augustus Leopold Egg. Number one from the trilogy known as *Past and Present*. London, Tate Gallery
11. Jean-Léon Gérôme. *The Artist's Model*. Haggin Collection, Haggin Museum, Stockton, California
12. Jules Breton. *The Song of the Lark*. Chicago Art Institute
13. Jean-François Millet. *The Gleaners*. Paris, Louvre
14. Käthe Kollwitz. *Losbruch* (Outbreak). Etching and aquatint
15. *La Femme émancipée repandant la lumière sur le monde* (a *pétroleuse*). Popular print
16. Diego Velázquez. *Rokeby Venus*. London, National Gallery
17. Hannah Höch. *Pretty Girl*. Hamburg, S. and G. Poppe Collection

vii

2 Morisot's *Wet Nurse:* The Construction of Work and Leisure in Impressionist Painting

3 Lost and *Found:* Once More the Fallen Woman

4 Some Women Realists

5 Florine Stettheimer: Rococo Subversive

6 Eroticism and Female Imagery in Nineteenth-Century Art

7 Why Have There Been No Great Women Artists?

Introduction

————

These essays have been written over the course of almost twenty years, twenty years which have seen the birth and development of a feminist art history. When I embarked on "Why Have There Been No Great Women Artists?" in 1970, there was no such thing as a feminist art history: like all other forms of historical discourse, it had to be constructed. New materials had to be sought out, a theoretical basis put in place, a methodology gradually developed. Since that time, feminist art history and criticism and, more recently, gender studies have become an important branch of the discipline, accorded the honor of a long and thorough review article in *The Art Bulletin,* a major journal of the discipline.[1] Perhaps more important, the feminist critique has entered into mainstream discourse itself: often, it is true, perfunctorily, but in the work of the best younger scholars, as an integral part of a new, more theoretically grounded and socially contextualized historical practice. Perhaps this makes it sound as though feminism is safely ensconced in the bosom of one of the most conservative of the intellectual disciplines.[2] This is far from being the case. There is still considerable resistance to the more radical varieties of the feminist critique in the visual arts, and its practitioners are accused of such sins as neglecting

————

the issue of quality, destroying the canon, scanting the innate visual dimension of the art work, reducing art to the context of its production—in other words, of undermining the ideological and, above all, aesthetic, biases of the discipline. All of this is to the good: feminist art history is there to make trouble, to call into question, to ruffle feathers in the patriarchal dovecotes. It should not be mistaken for just another variant of or supplement to mainstream art history. At its strongest, a feminist art history is a transgressive and anti-establishment practice, meant to call many of the major precepts of the discipline into question.

I have arranged these essays in more or less reverse chronological order so that the reader can begin with the most recent work, that which is closest to my present concerns, and then move back into the past, so that the earlier pieces assume, as it were, a certain historical distance in relation to the present. I have left them as they were when they originally appeared, despite the strong temptation to correct what I now know to be errors of fact or feel to be mistakes of interpretation. To do otherwise would be to falsify the historical record: these essays were, after all, written in specific historical contexts, in response to concrete problems and situations. I feel closer today to some of these essays than to others, and certainly, some of the earlier ones have been superseded in terms of theoretical sophistication and detailed scholarship by more recent work both in this country and abroad.[3] Nevertheless, there are, as the reader will discover, certain dominant themes and perspectives running through them, as well as a persistently critical attitude toward the practice of mainstream art history which provides a unity to the texts as a whole despite the range of subjects and approaches represented by the individual pieces.

Critique has always been at the heart of my project and remains there today. I do not conceive of a feminist art history as a positive approach to the field, a way of simply adding a token list of women painters and sculptors to the canon, although such recuperation of lost production and lost modes of productivity has its own historical validity and, as such, can function as part of the questioning of the conventional formulation of the parameters of the discipline. Even when discussing individual artists, like Florine Stettheimer or Berthe Morisot or Rosa Bonheur, it is not so much, or not merely, to validate their work—in the case of Rosa Bonheur, for instance, no such attempt has been made—but rather, in reading them, and often reading them against the grain, to question the whole art-historical apparatus which has contrived to "put them in their place"; in other words, to reveal the structures and operations that tend to marginalize certain kinds of artistic production while centralizing others. The role of ideology constantly appears as a motivating force in all such canon formation and as such has been a constant object of my critical attention, in the sense that such analysis "makes visible the invisible." Althusser's work on ideology is of course basic to such an undertaking, but, it will become clear, I am by no means a consistent Althusserian. On the contrary, I have paid considerable attention to other ways of formulating the notion of ideology and the role of the ideological in the visual arts.[4]

Finally, a few words about each of the individual essays, which I will take up in chronological order. "Why Have There Been No Great Women Artists?" was written during the heady days of the birth of the Women's Liberation movement, in 1970, and shares the political energy and the optimism of the period. It was at least partially based on research carried out the previous year, when I had conducted the first seminar, at Vassar College, on women and art. It was intended for publication in one of the earliest scholarly texts of the feminist movement, *Women in Sexist Society*, edited by V. Gornick and B. Moran (New York: Basic Books, 1971), but appeared first as a richly illustrated article in a pioneering, and controversial, number of *Art News* (vol. 69, January 1971), dedicated to women's issues.

The piece "Eroticism and Female Imagery in Nineteenth-Century Art" was originally written as the introduction to a session devoted to that subject I chaired at the meetings of the College Art Association in San Francisco in 1972. The picture of the male nude model holding a tray of bananas that accompanied this talk, my only essay in the realm of photography, created something of a sensation at the time, proving my point that the imagery of the erotic is gender-specific and nonreversible.[5]

"Some Women Realists" appeared originally as a two-part piece in *Arts Magazine* in 1974. I was extremely interested in contemporary realism at the time, partly as a result of my scholarly work on the nineteenth-century variety, and wanted to see if I could establish a specificity of feminine production within this mode of visual representation. I was also concerned to discredit essentialist notions about the existence of an atemporal, eternal "feminine" style, characterized by centralized imagery or delicate color, at the same time that I wished to demonstrate that the lived experience of women artists in a gendered society at a certain moment in history might lead in certain specific directions.

"Lost and *Found:* Once More the Fallen Woman," although it was published in *The Art Bulletin* in 1978, actually goes back to the Cook Lecture which I gave at the Institute of Fine Arts of New York University in the Spring of 1969 on Holman Hunt's *Awakening Conscience* and the image of the prostitute in British and French art of the later nineteenth century. In its present form, however, it was written for a symposium at Yale University in 1976, organized in conjunction with the exhibition *Dante Gabriel Rossetti and the Double Work of Art.* The symposium dealt with Rossetti as both poet *and painter,* and I took the rather unpopular position that Rossetti's poetry and painting were indeed vastly different in their formal structures, and that the unfinished *Found* was, among other things, a document of unreconstructed conservatism and hypocrisy.

"Florine Stettheimer: Rococo Subversive" first appeared in *Art in America* in 1980. By reading Stettheimer's work against the grain, as it were, I tried to call into question conventional notions of the nature of political art and, at the same time, to construct the artist's marginality as a woman and as a rejecter of both avant-garde and traditional positions in the art world of her time as a possible source of oppositional strength.

The two most recent articles, "Morisot's *Wet Nurse*: The Construction of Work and Leisure in Impressionist Painting" and "Women, Art, and Power" were conceived of as lectures before they were written up for this volume. The Morisot piece was given as a lecture at the exhibition of the work of Berthe Morisot at the National Gallery in Washington and at Mount Holyoke College in 1987 and 1988, respectively.

"Women, Art, and Power" has had a much longer, and a more metamorphic, history. It started life as a presentation at a symposium on narrativity and power at Rutgers University in 1979 (although in its present form it incorporates material going back as far as 1969 and as recent as last year), and I have been adding to it and changing it ever since. It is really based on the critical analysis of a large and varied, and ever-changing, number of representations of women, freely cannibalized from my own previous or current work, and which I have recontextualized for the purpose. There is no single "point" to the piece, although it is far from being without coherent organization, nor any reason why it should end where it does: in theory, it could go on forever. It is aimed at audiences of all kinds, and all levels of artistic and theoretical sophistication; it has been given all over the United States and in Europe—as far afield as Finland—and has been received with responses ranging from wild enthusiasm to baffled hostility, as well as with some helpful suggestions which I often took into account in constructing later versions. Although I have not footnoted them specifically, the work of such feminist art historians as Carol Duncan, Griselda Pollock, Eunice Lipton, Abigail Solomon-Godeau, and Maud Lavin has certainly informed my thought in this piece, as has the work of many feminist literary critics and theorists, feminist and otherwise, including that of my colleague Rosalind Krauss. "Women, Art, and Power" is meant as an ongoing and open-ended project, not as a finished piece. I prepared it for publication with a certain regret, knowing that it marked the end of an important era of my intellectual life, but also with a certain relief, knowing that I was now free to get on with other projects, to look to the future of the feminist reconstruction of the history of art.

The only other remarks that need to be made concern the illustrations. Obviously, they are not meant as anything more than reminders of the works in question, most of which may be found, in much better reproductions, in other, glossier publications.

Notes

1. See Thalia Gouma-Peterson and Patricia Mathews, "The Feminist Critique of Art History," *The Art Bulletin* LXIX, No. 3 (September 1987): 326–57. This article is an

excellent source of bibliography as well as a useful survey of the field.

2. The contrast between the welcome given to feminist production in the fields of literary history and criticism, as well as in historical studies, and its marginalization in that of art history is striking and worthy of further analysis.

3. See the copious bibliography provided by Gouma-Peterson and Mathews in *The Art Bulletin*, cited in note 1 above. English feminist art historians have been particularly productive and innovative in work premised on Marxist and psychoanalytic criticism. See especially the work of Rozsika Parker and Griselda Pollock, especially their now classic *Old Mistresses: Women, Art, and Ideology* (New York: Pantheon, 1981), and more recently, Kathleen Adler and Tamar Garb's *Berthe Morisot* (Ithaca, N.Y.: Cornell University Press, 1987); Lisa Tickner's *The Spectacle of Women: Imagery of the Suffrage Campaign, 1907–14* (London: Chatto & Windus, 1987); and Lynda Nead, *Myths of Sexuality: Representations of Women in Victorian Britain* (Oxford: Basil Blackwood, 1988). In this country, Eunice Lipton's *Looking into Degas: Uneasy Images of Women and Modern Life* (Berkeley, University of California Press, 1986) offers an example of the feminist critique of a single major artist of the nineteenth century.

4. For the basic formulation of a theory of ideology, see Louis Althusser, "Marxism and Humanism" (1965) in *For Marx* (Harmondsworth, England: Allen Lane, 1969) and "Ideology and Ideological State Apparatuses," in *Lenin and Philosophy* (London: New Left Books, 1971), and Tony Bennett, *Formalism and Marxism* (London and New York: Methuen), pp. 111–26. For a good critique of Althusser's notion of ideology in relation to literature, see Bennett, pp. 127–75.

5. "Eroticism and Female Imagery in Nineteenth-Century Art" was published in *Women as Sex-Object*, ed. Thomas B. Hess and Linda Nochlin (New York: Newsweek Books, 1972).

Women, Art, and Power

I

Women, Art, and Power

———

In this essay, I shall be investigating the relationships existing among women, art, and power in a group of visual images from the late eighteenth through the twentieth centuries. These visual images have been chosen for the most part because they represent women in situations involving power—most usually its lack. It is obvious that the story or content or narratives of these images—what art historians call their "iconography"—will be an important element for analysis in this project: the story of the Horatii represented by David, that of the death of Sardanapalus depicted by Delacroix; or the sad, exemplary tale of domestic downfall and punishment bodied forth by the English painter Augustus Egg in his pictorial trilogy known as *Past and Present*. [1]

Yet what I am really interested in are the operations of power on the level of ideology, operations which manifest themselves in a much more diffuse, more absolute, yet paradoxically more elusive sense, in what might be called the discourses of gender difference. I refer, of course, to the ways in which representations of women in art are founded upon and serve to reproduce indisputably accepted assumptions held by society in general, artists in particular, and some artists more than others about men's power over, superior-

———

ity to, difference from, and necessary control of women, assumptions which are manifested in the visual structures as well as the thematic choices of the pictures in question. Ideology manifests itself as much by what is unspoken—unthinkable, unrepresentable—as by what is articulated in a work of art. Insofar as many of the assumptions about women presented themselves as a complex of commonsense views about the world, and were therefore assumed to be self-evident, they were relatively invisible to most contemporary viewers, as well as to the creators of the paintings. Assumptions about women's weakness and passivity; her sexual availability for men's needs; her defining domestic and nurturing function; her identity with the realm of nature; her existence as object rather than creator of art; the patent ridiculousness of her attempts to insert herself actively into the realm of history by means of work or engagement in political struggle—all of these notions, themselves premised on an even more general, more all-pervasive certainty about gender difference itself—all of these notions were shared, if not uncontestedly, to a greater or lesser degree by most people of our period, and as such constitute an ongoing subtext underlying almost all individual images involving women. Yet perhaps the term "subtext" is misleading in view of my intentions. It is not a *deep* reading I am after; this is not going to be an attempt to move *behind* the images into some realm of more profound truth lurking beneath the surface of the various pictorial texts. My attempt to investigate the triad woman-art-power should rather be thought of as an effort to disentangle various discourses about power related to gender difference existing simultaneously with—as much surface as substratum—the master discourse of the iconography or narrative.

It is important to keep in mind that one of the most important functions of ideology is to veil the overt power relations obtaining in society at a particular moment in history by making them appear to be part of the natural, eternal order of things. It is also important to remember that symbolic power is invisible and can be exercised only with the complicity of those who fail to recognize either that they submit to it or that they exercise it. Women artists are often no more immune to the blandishments of ideological discourses than their male contemporaries, nor should dominant males be envisioned as conspiratorially or even consciously forcing their notions upon women. Michel Foucault has reflected that power is tolerable "only on the condition that it mask a considerable part of itself."[2] The patriarchal discourse of power over women masks itself in the veil of the natural—indeed, of the logical.

Strength and weakness are understood to be the natural corollaries of gender difference. Yet it is more accurate to say, in a work like David's *Oath of the Horatii* [1], that it is the representation of gender differences—male versus female—that immediately establishes that opposition between strength and weakness which is the point of the picture.

In the *Horatii*, the notion of woman's passivity—and her propensity to give in to personal feeling—would appear to have existed for the artist as an available element of a visual *langue* upon which the high intelligibility of this specific pictorial *parole* depends. It is

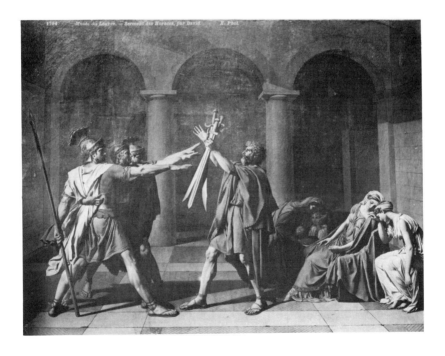

1. Jacques-Louis David. *The Oath of the Horatii*

important to realize that the particular narrative incident represented here—the moment when the three brothers, the Horatii, take
a patriotic oath of allegiance to Rome on swords held before them
by their father in the presence of the women and children of the
family—is not to be found in Classical or post-Classical texts, but is
in essence a Davidian invention, arrived at after many other explora-
tions of potential subjects from the story.[3] It is an invention which
owes its revolutionary clarity precisely to the clear-cut opposition
between masculine strength and feminine weakness offered by the
ideological discourse of the period. The striking effectiveness of the
visual communication here depends in the most graphic way possible upon a universal assumption: it is not something that needs to
be thought about. The binary division here between male energy,
tension, and concentration as opposed to female resignation, flac-
cidity, and relaxation is as clear as any Lévi-Straussian diagram of
a native village; it is carried out in every detail of pictorial structure
and treatment, is inscribed on the bodies of the protagonists in their
poses and anatomy, and is even evident in the way that the male
figures are allotted the lions' share of the architectural setting, expanding to fill it, whereas the women, collapsed in upon themselves,
must make do with a mere corner. So successful is the binary division of male versus female in conveying David's message about the
superior claims of duty to the state over personal feeling that we
tend to consider a later version of *The Oath of the Horatii*, like that
by Armand Caraffe,[4] to be weak and confusing at least in part
because it fails to rely on the clear-cut "natural" opposition which
is the basis of David's clarity.

In the middle of the nineteenth century, in Victorian England,
woman's passivity, her defining inability to defend herself against
physical violence, would appear to have been such an accepted
article of faith that the poses which had signified weakness—the
very opposite of heroism in David's *Horatii*—could now, with a bit
of neck straightening and chin stiffening, in the case of British
ladies, be read as heroism itself. Indeed, Sir Joseph Noel Paton, the
author of such a work, which appeared in the 1858 Royal Academy
show under the title *In Memoriam* [2] (the original has disappeared),
dedicated it "to Commemorate the Christian Heroism of the British

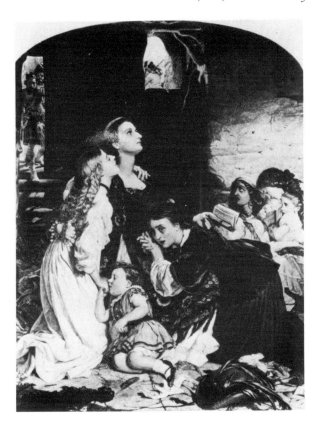

2. Sir Joseph Noel Paton. *In Memoriam.* Engraving after the lost original painting

Ladies in India during the Mutiny of 1857." It must be added parenthetically that the figures entering so energetically from the rear were originally not the Scottish rescuers we see in the engraving after the painting, but rather those of bloodthirsty Sepoys, the Indian rebels, which were altered because the artist felt their presence created "too painful an impression."[5] The heroism of British ladies would seem to have consisted of kneeling down and allowing themselves and their children to be atrociously raped and murdered, dressed in the most unsuitably fashionable but flattering clothes possible, without lifting a finger to defend themselves. Yet to admiring spectators of the time, tranquility and the Bible, rather than

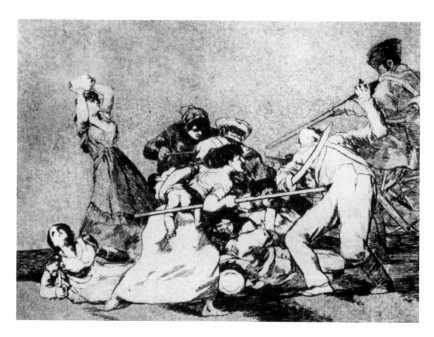

3. Francisco Goya y Lucientes. *And They Are Like Wild Beasts.*
Etching and aquatint

vigorous self-defense, were precisely what constituted heroism for
a lady. Said the reviewer in the *Art Journal* of the time: "The
spectator is fascinated by the sublimely calm expression of the prin-
cipal head—hers is more than Roman virtue; her lips are parted in
prayer; she holds the Bible in her hand, and that is her strength."[6]
Now there are at least two discourses articulated in this image. One
is the overt story of heroic British ladies and their children during
the Sepoy mutiny, fortifying themselves with prayer as they are
about to be assaulted by savage, and presumably lustful, natives. The
other discourse, less obvious, is the patriarchal and class-defined one
which stipulates the appropriate behavior for the lady, and it implies
that no lady will ever unsex herself by going so far as to raise a hand
in physical violence, even in defense of her children. Such a notion
about ladylike or "womanly" behavior had of course some but not
necessarily a great deal of relationship to how women, British ladies
during the Sepoy mutiny included, have actually acted under simi-

lar circumstances.[7] Goya's women, in the etching *And They Are Like Wild Beasts* from the "Disasters of War" series [3], though obviously not ladies, are shown behaving quite differently from those in *In Memoriam*, although the fact that these peasant women resort to violence itself functions as a sign of the extremity of the situation. The Spanish mothers who fight so desperately to defend their children, it is implied, are something other than women: they "are like wild beasts."[8]

The suffragists, at the beginning of the twentieth century, attempted, as the photograph in Figure 4 reveals,[9] to create a convincing image of women combining ladylike decorum *and* overt physi-

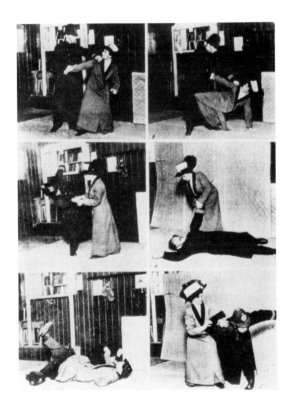

4. *Woman Toppling Policeman with a Jujitsu Throw.* Photograph

cal power. The results—a properly dressed young woman toppling a startled policeman with a jujitsu throw—hover between the invigorating and the ludicrous. The discourse of power and the code of ladylike behavior can maintain only an unstable relationship: the two cannot mix.

The success of a discourse in confirming an ideological position rests not in its reliance upon evidence but rather in the way it exercises successful control through the "obviousness" of its assumptions. Force, to borrow the words of Talcott Parsons, rather than being the *characteristic* feature, is, in fact, a special limiting case of the deployment of power;[10] coercion represents the regression of power to a lower domain of generalization; a "show of force" is the emblematic sign of the failure of power's *symbolic* currency.[11] Nevertheless, Victorian assumptions about ladylike behavior are premised on the kinds of threats that, although rarely mentioned, lie in store for those who call them into question: the woman who goes so far as to rely on physical force or independent action is no longer to be considered a lady. It then follows that because women are so naturally defenseless and men so naturally aggressive, real ladies must depend not on themselves but on male defenders—as in *In Memoriam*, the Scottish troops, to protect them from (similarly male) attackers, the (overpainted) Sepoy mutineers.

That these views were held to be self-evident by both men and women at the time goes without saying: ideology is successful precisely to the degree that its views are shared by those who exercise power and those who submit to it. But there is a corollary to the assumptions underlying the visual text here which would have been more available to men than to women: what one might call its fantasy potential—a discourse of desire—the imaginative construction of a sequel to *In Memoriam*: something like *The Rape and Murder of the British Women During the Indian Mutiny*, a subject current in the popular press of the period. It is this aspect of the painting, its hint of "unspeakable things to come," delicately referred to in the contemporary review as "those fiendish atrocities [which] cannot be borne without a shudder,"[12] which must have in part accounted for its popularity with the public.

This sort of sequel does, of course, exist, although it predates

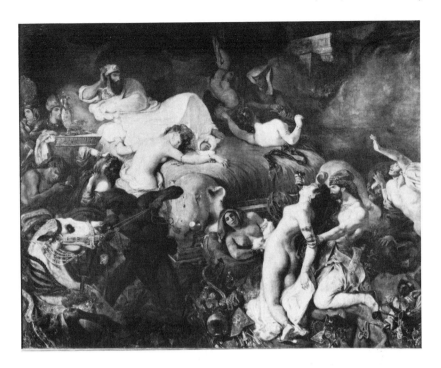

5. Eugène Delacroix. *The Death of Sardanapalus*

In Memoriam and was painted in France rather than in England: Delacroix's *Death of Sardanapalus* [5]. "In dreams begin responsibilities," a poet has said.[13] Perhaps. Certainly, one is on surer footing asserting that in power dreams begin—dreams of still greater power, in this case, fantasies of men's limitless power to enjoy, by destroying them, the bodies of women. Delacroix's painting cannot, of course, be reduced to a mere pictorial projection of the artist's sadistic fantasies under the guise of exoticism. Yet one must keep in mind that subtending the vivid turbulence of the text of Delacroix's story—the story of the ancient Assyrian ruler Sardanapalus, who, upon hearing of his incipient defeat, had all his precious possessions, including his women, destroyed, and then went up in flames with them in his palace—lies the more mundane assumption, shared by men of Delacroix's class, that they were naturally "entitled" to desire, to possess, and to control the bodies of women. If the men were artists, it was assumed that they had more or less unlimited access to the bodies of the women who worked for them as models. In other words, Delacroix's private fantasy exists not in a vacuum but in a particular social context, granting permission as well as establishing boundaries for certain kinds of behavior. It is almost impossible to imagine a *Death of Cleopatra*, say, with nude male slaves being put to death by women servants, painted by a *woman* artist of this period. In the sexual power system of patriarchy, transgression is not merely that which violates understood codes of thought and behavior: it is, even more urgently, that which marks their farthest boundaries. Sexual transgression may be understood as a *threshold* of permissible behavior—actual, imaginary—rather than as its opposite. The true site of opposition is marked by gender difference.

Delacroix attempted to defuse and distance his overt expression of man's total domination of women in a variety of ways, at the same time that he emphasized the sexually provocative aspects of his theme. He engaged in the carnage by placing at the blood-red heart of the picture a surrogate self—the recumbent Sardanapalus on his bed—but a self who holds himself aloof from the sensual tumult which surrounds him, an artist-destroyer who is ultimately to be consumed in the flames of his own creation-destruction.

Despite the brilliant feat of artistic semi-sublimation pulled off here, the public and critics were apparently appalled by the work when it first appeared, in the Salon of 1828.[14] The aloofness of the hero of the piece fooled no one, really. Although criticism was generally directly more against the painting's formal failings, it is obvious that by depicting such a subject with such obvious sensual relish, such erotic *panache* and such openness, Delacroix had come too close to an overt statement of the most explosive, hence the most carefully repressed, fantasy of the patriarchal discourse of desire: the Sadean identification of murder and sexual possession as an assertion of absolute *jouissance*.

The fantasy of absolute possession of women's naked bodies, a fantasy which for the nineteenth-century artist was at least in part a reality in terms of specific practice—the constant availability of studio models for sexual as well as professional needs—lies at the heart of less-inspired pictorial representations of Near Eastern or

Classical themes, such as Jean-Léon Gérôme's *Oriental Slave Market* [6]. In this case, of course, an iconographical representation of power relations coincides with, although it is not identical to, assumptions about male authority. Although ostensibly realistic representations of the customs of picturesque Orientals,[15] Gérôme's paintings are also suitably veiled affirmations of the fact that women are actually for sale to men for the latter's sexual satisfaction—in Paris just as in the Near East. Sexual practice is more successfully ideologized in this case than in Delacroix's painting, and works like

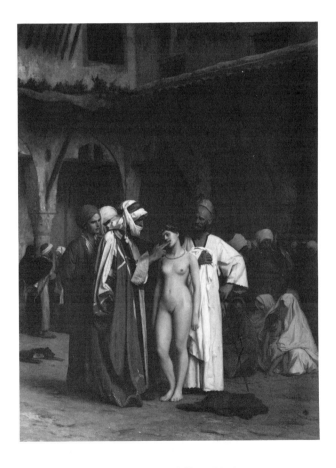

6. Jean-Léon Gérôme. *Oriental Slave Market*

these appeared frequently in the Salons of the period, and were much admired. Why was this the case? First of all, on the level of formal structure, they were more acceptable because Gérôme has substituted a chilly and remote pseudo-scientific naturalism—small, self-effacing brushstrokes, "rational" and convincing spatial effects (an apparently dispassionate empiricism)—for Delacroix's tempestuous self-involvement, the impassioned brio of his paint surfaces. Gérôme's style justifies his subject (if not to us, who are cannier readers, certainly to most of the spectators of his time), by guaranteeing through sober "objectivity" the unassailable Otherness of the characters enacting his narrative. He is saying in effect: "Don't think that I, or any other right-thinking Frenchman, would ever be involved in this sort of thing. I am merely taking careful note of the fact that less enlightened races indulge in the trade in naked women —but isn't it arousing!" Gérôme is, like many other artists of his time, managing to body forth a double message here: one about men's power over women and the other about white man's superiority to, hence justifiable control over, darker races—precisely those who indulge in this sort of lascivious trade. Or one might say that something more complex is involved in Gérôme's strategies here vis-à-vis the *homme moyen sensuel*: the latter was invited sexually to identify with yet at the same time morally to distance himself from his Oriental counterparts within the objectively inviting yet racially distancing space of the painting.

Édouard Manet's *Ball at the Opera* of 1873 [7] may, for the purposes of my argument, be read as a combative response to and subversion of both the manifest and latent content of Gérôme's slave markets.[16] Like Gérôme's painting, Manet's, in the words of Julius Meier-Graefe, represents a "flesh market."[17] Unlike Gérôme, however, Manet represented the marketing of attractive women not in a suitably distanced Near Eastern locale but behind the galleries of the Opera House on the rue Lepeltier; and the buyers of female flesh were not Oriental louts but, rather, civilized and recognizable Parisian men-about-town, Manet's friends and, in some cases, fellow artists whom he had asked to pose for him. Unlike Gérôme's painting, which had been accepted for the Salon of 1867, Manet's was rejected for that of 1874. I should like to suggest that the reason for

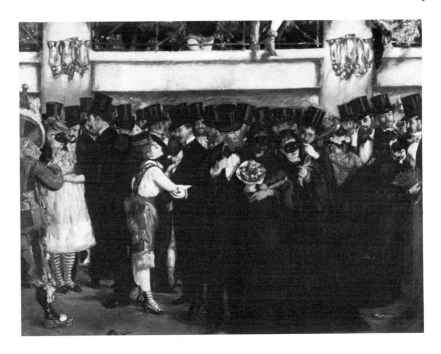

7. Édouard Manet. *The Ball at the Opera*

Manet's rejection was neither merely the daring close-to-homeness of his representation of feminine sexual availability and male consumption of it nor merely, as his friend and defender at the time, Stéphane Mallarmé suggested, its formal daring—its deliberate yet casual-looking cut-off view of the spectacle[18]—but rather the way these two kinds of subversive impulses interact.

It is precisely Manet's anti-narrative strategies in the construction of the painting, his refusal of transparency, that renders the ideological assumptions of his times unstable. By rejecting traditional modes of pictorial storytelling, by interrupting the flow of narrative with cut-off legs and torso at the top of the painting and a cut-off male figure to the left, Manet's painting reveals the assumptions on which such narratives are premised. The detached parts of female bodies constitute a witty rhetorical reference, a substitution of part for whole, to the sexual availability of lower-class and marginal women for the pleasure of upper-class men. By means of a

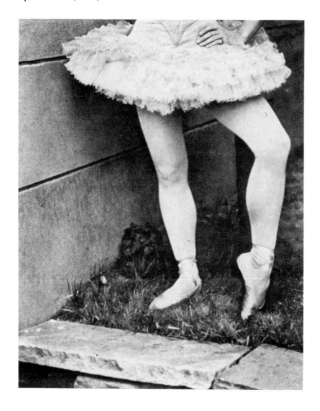

8. André Kertesz. *Dancer's Legs.* Photograph

brilliant realist strategy, Manet has at once made us aware of the artifice of art, as opposed to Gérôme's pseudo-scientific denial of it with his illusionistic naturalism, and, at the same time, through the apparently accidentally amputated legs, of the nature of the power relations controlling the worldly goings-on here. Later, in Manet's *Bar at the Folies-Bergère* of 1881, the device of the cut-off legs appears again in the representation of a working woman, the barmaid, to remind us of the nature of the discreet negotiations going on between the foreground figure and the shadowy man reflected in the mirror, and at the same time to call attention to the arbitrariness of the boundaries of the frame. The image of the cut-off leg offers an easily grasped, nontransferable synecdoche of sexual power relations. When the image is feminine, as it is in André Kertesz's well-known photograph of a dancer's legs of 1939 [8], it inevitably refers to the implied sexual attractiveness of the invisible model, presented as a passive object for the male gaze. This is never the implication of similarly fragmented masculine legs, whether they be those of the ascending Christ in a medieval manuscript or those of an avenging hero in a modern comic strip.[19] If the fragmented legs are masculine, they consistently function as signifiers of energy and power.

Within the implicit context of passivity, sexual availability, and helplessness, how might a respectable woman artist in England in the middle of the nineteenth century create a convincing image of her professional situation? Not very easily or very convincingly. Indeed, it has been hard for viewers to tell that Emily Mary Osborn's painting *Nameless and Friendless* [9] is in fact a representation of a woman artist. The subject was defined as "A Gentlewoman

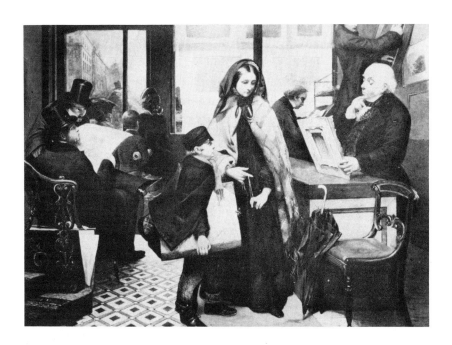

9. Emily Mary Osborn. *Nameless and Friendless*

reduced to dependence upon her brother's art" in the 1970 edition of *The History and Philosophy of Art Education.* [20] Yet the documentary evidence, as well as a careful reading of the pictorial text, points to the fact that Osborn intended this as the representation of a young, orphaned woman artist offering her work with considerable anxiety to a skeptical picture dealer.[21] It is then to some extent a self-image of the woman artist who painted it, clothed in the language of British genre painting. Even the briefest inspection of the accepted codes for the representation of artists and the accepted codes for the representation of respectable young ladies at the time reveals at once why a spectator might misinterpret the work and why Osborn might have chosen this somewhat ambiguous iconography for her representation of the woman artist.

One might well assume that Osborn, as a canny and popular purveyor of acceptable genre painting to the Victorian public, shared the "natural" assumptions of the Royal Academy's public that the proper setting for a respectable young woman was that of home and family. She also, no doubt, shared the assumptions controlling the first canvas of Augustus Leopold Egg's trilogy [10] about a respectable married woman's fall and expulsion from home. An independent life, a life outside the home, was all too often, for the gentlewoman above all, related to potential sexual availability and, of course, understood to be the punishment for sexual lapse in the narrative codes of the time. Indeed, there is more than a hint, conveyed by the ogling loungers to the left of Osborn's picture, who lift their eyes from a print of a scantily clad dancing girl to scrutinize the young woman artist, that merely being out in the world at all rather than safely home opens a young, unprotected woman to suspicion. It becomes clearer why Osborn has chosen to define the situation of the woman artist as one of plight rather than of power. Only dire necessity would, she implies, force a young woman out into the dangerous public arena of professionalism. The narrative of the woman artist is here cautiously founded on a pictorial discourse of vulnerability—of powerlessness, in short. Osborn's woman artist, in her exposure to the male gaze within the painting, is positioned more in the expected situation of the female *model* than that of the male artist.

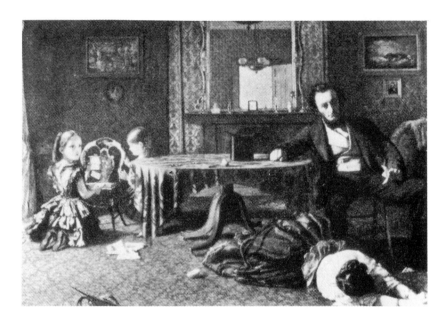

10. Augustus Leopold Egg. Number one from the trilogy known as
Past and Present

By no stretch of the imagination can one envisage a woman
artist of the nineteenth century interpreting her role, as did her male
counterparts quite freely and naturally, in terms of free access to the
naked bodies of the opposite sex. Gérôme, on the contrary, in his
self-portrait *The Artist's Model* [11] has simply depicted himself in
one of the most conventionally acceptable and, indeed, self-explana-
tory narrative structures for the self-representation of the artist. The
topos of the artist in his studio assumes that being an artist has to
do with man's free access to naked women. Art-making, the very
creation of beauty itself, was equated with the representation of the
female nude. Here, the very notion of the originary power of the
artist, his status as creator of unique and valuable objects, is founded
on a discourse of gender difference as power.

This assumption is presented quite overtly, although with a
certain amount of tactful, naturalistic hedging, in *The Artist's Model*.
The artist does not represent himself touching the *living woman* on
her thigh, but only her plaster representation, with gloved hands;

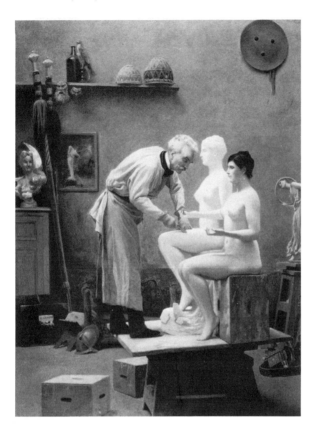

11. Jean-Léon Gérôme. *The Artist's Model*

and the artist himself is (conveniently for the purposes of the painting) white-haired and venerable rather than young and lusty. He
may remind us more of a doctor than an artist, and he keeps his eyes
modestly lowered on his work, rather than raising them to confront
the naked woman. The overt iconography here is the perfectly
acceptable theme of the artist in his studio, industriously and
single-mindedly engaging in creative activity, surrounded by tes-
timonials to his previous achievements. Assumptions about masculine power are perfectly and disarmingly justified by the noble
purposes which this power serves: although the naked model may
indeed serve the purposes of the artist, he in turn is merely the

humble servant of a higher cause, that of Beauty itself. This complex of beliefs involving male power, naked models, and the creation of art receives its most perfect rationalization in the ever-popular nineteenth-century representation of the Pygmalion myth: stone beauty made flesh by the warming glow of masculine desire.

Nowhere is the work of ideology more evident than when issues of class join with issues of gender in the production of female imagery. In the case of the peasant woman, the association of the rural female with a timeless, nurturing, aesthetically distancing realm of nature served to defuse her potentiality—indeed, her actuality, in France, where the memory of women armed with pitchforks still hovered like a nightmare—as a political threat. The assimilation of the peasant woman to the realm of nature helped to rationalize rural poverty and the farm woman's continual grinding labor, as well as to justify her subjugation to a tradition of male tyranny within peasant culture itself.

Works like Giovanni Segantini's *Two Mothers* (see Chapter 2, Figure 2), with its overt connection between the nurturing functions of cow and woman, make clear the presuppositions of an ideology which supports motherhood as woman's "naturally" ordained work and demonstrates, at the same time, that the *peasant* woman, as an elemental, untutored—hence eminently "natural"— female, is the ideal signifier for the notion of beneficent maternity, replete with historical overtones of the Christian Madonna and Child.

The peasant woman also served as the natural vehicle for uplifting notions about religious faith. In works like Alphonse LeGros's *Ex-Voto* or Wilhelm Leibl's *Peasant Women in the Church,* piety is viewed as a natural concomitant of edifying fatalism, as is the peasant woman's conservative instinct to perpetuate unquestioningly traditional religious practices from generation to generation.

Yet contradictorily—ideology of course, functioning to absorb and rationalize contradiction—at the same time that the peasant woman is represented as naturally nurturing and pious, her very naturalness, her proximity to instinct and animality, could make the image of the female peasant serve as the very embodiment of untrammeled, unartificed sexuality. Sometimes this sexual force may

be veiled in idealization, as in the work of Jules Breton, who specialized in glamorizing and classicizing the erotic charms of the peasant
girl for the annual Salon and the delectation of American midwest-
ern nouveau-riche collectors [12]; sometimes it was served up more
crudely and overtly, but the peasant woman's "natural" role as a
signifier of earthy sensuality is as important an element in the nineteenth-century construction of gender as her nurturant or religious
roles.

Nowhere does the assimilation of the peasant woman to the
realm of nature receive more effective pictorial representation than
in Millet's famous *Gleaners* of 1857 [13].[22] Here, the genuinely prob-

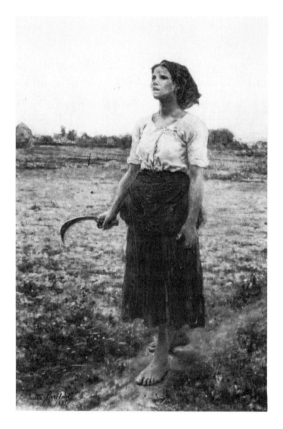

12. Jules Breton. *The Song of the Lark*

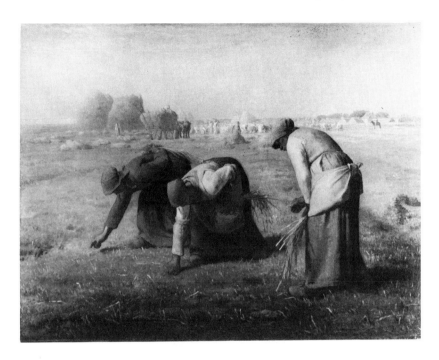

13. Jean-François Millet. *The Gleaners*

lematic implications surrounding the issue of gleaning—traditionally the way the poorest, weakest members of rural society obtained
their bread and an area in which women had, in fact, historically
played a relatively active role as participants in the recurrent disturb-
ances connected with the rights of *glanage*[23]—have been transformed into a Realist version of the pastoral. Although overwrought
conservative critics of the time may have seen the specter of revolution hovering behind the three bent figures, a cooler reading of the
pictorial text reveals that Millet was, on the contrary, unwilling to
emphasize the potentiality for an expression of genuine social conflict implied by the contrast between the richness of the harvest of
the wealthy landowner in the background and the poverty of the
gleaning figures in the foreground.[24] Rather, Millet chose, by enno-
bling the poses and assimilating the figures to Biblical and Classical
prototypes, to remove them from the politically charged context of

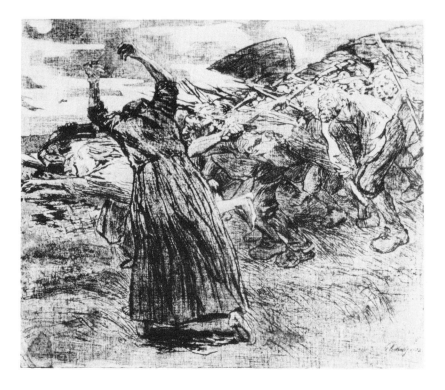

14. Käthe Kollwitz. *Losbruch* (Outbreak). Etching and aquatint

contemporary history and to place them in the suprahistoric context of High Art. At the same time, through the strategies of his composition, Millet makes it clear that this particularly unrewarding labor must be read as ordained by nature itself rather than brought about by specific conditions of historical injustice. Indeed, the very fact that the workers in question are *glaneuses* rather than *glaneurs* makes their situation more acceptable; as women, they slide more easily into a position of identity with the natural order. Millet emphasizes this woman-nature connection in a specific aspect of his composition: the bodies of the bending women are quite literally encompassed and limited by the boundaries of the earth itself.[25] It is as though the earth imprisons them, not feudalism or capitalism.

As a visual affirmation of feminine self-assertiveness and power, Käthe Kollwitz's *Losbruch* [14]—*Outbreak* or *Revolt*—offers the most startling contrast to Millet's *Gleaners*. An etching of 1903 from the artist's "Peasants' War" series, the image can be seen as a kind of "anti-*glaneuses*," a counter-pastoral, with the dynamic, vertical thrust of its angular female protagonist, who galvanizes the crowd behind her, serving to subvert the message of passive acquiescence to the "natural" order created by Millet's composition. One might say that what Millet scrupulously avoided by resorting to the peasant woman in his representation, Kollwitz openly asserts through her: rage, energy, action.

Kollwitz turned for historical as well as pictorial inspiration for her dominating figure of Black Anna, a leader of the sixteenth-century peasant uprising, to Wilhelm Zimmermann's classical account, *The Great German Peasants' War*, which described this powerful woman and provided a popular woodcut illustration of her as well.[26] No doubt Delacroix's classical revolutionary image, *Liberty at the Barricades*, lingered in the back of Kollwitz's mind when she created her print. But the difference is, of course, that Delacroix's powerful figure of Liberty is, like almost all such feminine embodiments of human virtue—Justice, Truth, Temperance, Victory—an allegory rather than a concrete historical woman, an example of what Simone de Beauvoir has called Woman-as-Other. The figure of Black Anna, on the contrary, is historically specific and meant to serve as a concrete locus of identification for the viewer. By introducing the back-view figure of a powerful woman-of-the-people into the foreground of the scene, the artist attempts to persuade the viewer to identify with the event, as she herself does.[27] Kollwitz, who sympathized with both feminism and socialism at this time and was particularly impressed by August Bebel's pioneering document of feminism, *Woman Under Socialism*, specifically identified herself with Black Anna. She told her biographer that "she had portrayed herself in this woman. She wanted the signal to attack to come from her."[28] In *Outbreak*, perhaps for the first time, a woman artist has attempted to challenge the assumptions of gender ideology, piercing through the structure of symbolic domination with conscious, politically informed awareness.

It is also significant that Kollwitz selected a narrative of outright social disorder for the representation of a powerful, energetic female figure, directing rather than submitting to the action of her fellows. The topos of woman on top, to borrow the title of Natalie Zemon Davis's provocative study of sex-role reversal in preindustrial Europe, has always been a potent, if often humorous, image of unthinkable disorder.[29] Generally during our period, gestures of power and self-affirmation, especially of political activism, on the part of women were treated with special visual viciousness. Daumier, in a lithograph subtitled "V'la une femme qui à l'heure solonelle où nous sommes, s'occupe bêtement avec ses enfants," created in 1848, the very year of the democratic revolution fought in the name of greater equality, treated the two feminists to the left of the print (recognizable caricatures of two prominent activists of the time) as denatured hags, saggy, scrawny, uncorseted creatures, whose dissatisfied gracelessness contrasted vividly with the unself-conscious charm of the little mother to the right, who continued to care for her child heedless of the tumult of history.[30] The working-class women activists of the Commune, the so-called *pétroleuses* [15], were mercilessly caricatured by the Government of Order as frightening, subhuman, witchlike creatures, demons of destruction intent on literally destroying the very fabric of the social order by burning down buildings.[31]

In the sixteenth century, Pieter Brueghel had used the figure of a powerful, active woman, Dulle Griet, or Mad Meg, to signify contemporary spiritual and political disorder. Indeed, it is possible that Kollwitz herself may have turned to this, one of the most potent images of the menace of the unleashed power of women, for her conception of Black Anna in the "Peasants' War" series, an image more or less contemporary with her subject: Mad Meg, who, with her band of ferocious female followers, served as the very emblem of fiery destruction and disorder, a visual summary of the reversal of the proper power relations and the natural hierarchy of a well-ordered world, to borrow the words of Natalie Zemon Davis.[32] For the sixteenth century, as for the nineteenth, the most potent natural signifier possible for folly and chaos was woman unleashed, self-determined, definitely on top: this was the only image sufficiently destructive of "normal" power relations, rich enough in negative significations, to indicate the destruction of value itself.

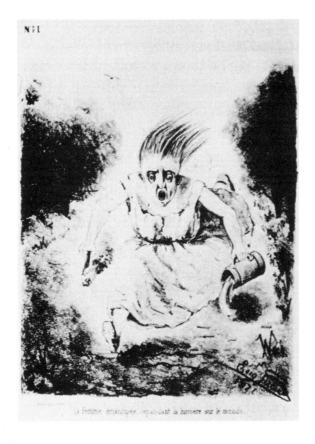

15. *La Femme émancipée repandant la lumière sur le monde* (a *pétroleuse*). Popular print

In the figure of Black Anna, Kollwitz has transvaluated the values of Mad Meg, so to speak, and made them into positive if frightening visual signifiers.[33] The dark, chthonic force associated with the peasant woman, those malevolent, sometimes supernatural powers associated with the unleashing of feminine, popular energies and not totally foreign to the most menacing of all female figures —the witch—here assumes a positive social and psychological value: the force of darkness, in the context of historic consciousness, is transformed into a harbinger of light.

On March 10, 1914, approximately ten years after Kollwitz had created her image of woman's power, a militant suffragist, Mary Richardson, alias Polly Dick, took an axe to Velázquez's *Rokeby Venus* in the National Gallery in London [16]. It was an act of aesthetic destruction comparable in the strength of its symbolic significance to Courbet's supposed destruction of the Vendôme column during the Commune, and was greeted with a similar sort of public outrage. Mary Richardson declared that she had tried to destroy the picture of the most beautiful woman in mythological history as a protest against the government for destroying Mrs. Pankhurst, who was the most beautiful character in modern history. The fact that she disliked the painting had made it easier for her to carry out her daring act.[34] Richardson's vandalism quite naturally created a public furor at the time: she had dared to destroy public property, ruined a priceless masterpiece, wielded a dangerous weapon in an art gallery. Even today, the right-thinking art lover

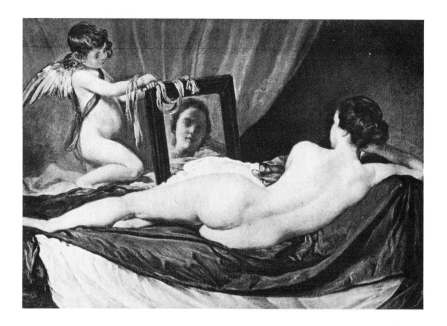

16. Diego Velázquez. *Rokeby Venus*

must shudder at the thought of the blade hacking through Velázquez's image, through no mere accident the very image of Beauty itself. We may find Mary Richardson admirable for acting courageously, engaging in a punishable act for a political cause she deemed worth fighting for, and attempting to destroy a work she believed stood for everything she, as a militant suffragist, detested, yet it is clear that she was also wrong. Wrong because her act was judged to be that of a vicious madwoman and did the suffrage cause little or no good; but more than that, wrong in that her gesture assumes that if the cause of women's rights is right, then Velázquez's *Venus* is wrong. Yet it also may be said, as Jacqueline Rose has in her article "Sexuality in the Field of Vision," that "if the visual image, in its aesthetically acclaimed form, serves to maintain a particular and oppressive mode of sexual recognition, it nevertheless does so only partially."[35] Is it then possible to respond differentially to the image of Venus?

Over and above our specialized reactions to the *Rokeby Venus's* unique qualities of shape, texture, and color, and yet because of these qualities, we may respond to a variety of other kinds of suggestions generated by the painting: suggestions of human loveliness, physical tenderness, and the pleasure both sexes take in sensual discovery and self-discovery; we may also, if we are past youth and up on our iconography, be reminded of the swift passage of beauty and pleasure and the vanity of all such delights, visual and otherwise, suggested in the painting by the topos of the woman with a mirror: *vanitas.* Here, the mirror brings us not only an adumbration of mysterious beauty but, at the same time, intimations of its inevitable destruction. Such readings are possible either if we are totally unaware of the power relations obtaining between men and women inscribed in visual representation; or, if we have become aware of them, we choose to ignore them while we enjoy or otherwise respond positively to the image in question; or, if we cannot ignore them, feel that we are in no way affected by them.

The question whether it is possible at this point in history for women simply to "appreciate" the female nude in some simple and unproblematic way leads us to ask the question whether any positive visual representation of women is possible at all. A photocollage,

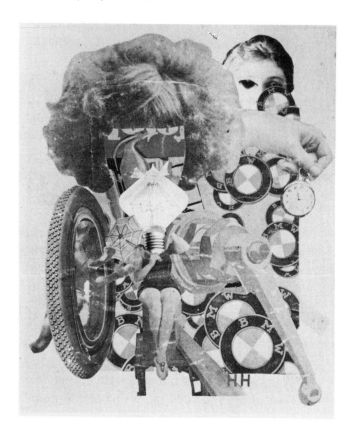

17. Hannah Höch. *Pretty Girl*

Pretty Girl (Das schöne Mädchen), of 1920 [17] by Hannah Höch, a member of Berlin Dada, suggests "in Utopia, yes; under patriarchy, in a consumer society, no." Höch's photocollage reminds us of another kind of cutting practice in art besides the destructive one of Polly Dick: deconstructive and instructive. Obviously Höch's cut-ups offer an alternative to the slicing up of Velázquez's nude, another way of refusing the image of woman as a transcendent object of art and the male gaze, generator of a string of similarly depoliticized art objects. This deconstructive practice of art—or anti-art—reveals that any representation of woman as sexual object, far from being natural or simply "given," is itself a construction. If

traditional representation has insisted upon maintaining the spectator within "an illusorily unfissured narrative space,"[36] then it hardly
seems an accident that the material practice of photocollage, that
free and aggressive combination of words and ready-made images
characteristic of Berlin Dada in the 1920s, manifests its subversive
politics in an act of cutting down and reconstructing, in which the
original deconstructive impulse remains assertively revealed in the
deliberate crudeness, discontinuity, and lack of logical coherence of
the structure of the work. A photocollage like Hannah Höch's
Pretty Girl, made out of ready-made materials, denies the "original-
ity" or "creativity" of the masterful male artist vis-à-vis his female
subject. It denies the beauty of the beautiful woman as object of the
gaze and at the same time insists on the finished work as the result
of a process of production—cutting and pasting—rather than inspiration. *Pretty Girl* is in part a savagely funny attack on mass-produced standards of beauty, the narcissism stimulated by the media
to keep women unproblematically self-focused. At the same time,
the collage allegorizes the arbitrarily constructed quality of *all* representations of beauty: the "pretty girl" of the title is clearly a
product assembled from products—it is the opposite of the *belle
peinture* of the *belle créature.* Hannah Höch, previously considered
"marginal" within the context of Berlin Dada, now assumes a more
central position in light of the work of contemporary women image-
makers concerned with the problematics of gendered representation. Barbara Kruger, Cindy Sherman, Mary Kelly, and many others are again cutting into the fabric of representation by refusing any
kind of simple "mirroring" of female subjects; they turn to collage,
photomontage, self-indexical photography, combinations of texts,
images, and objects as ways of calling attention to the production
of gender itself—its inscription in the unconscious—as a social construction rather than a natural phenomenon.

What of women as spectators or consumers of art? The acceptance of woman as object of the desiring male gaze in the visual arts
is so universal that for a woman to question, or to draw attention
to this fact, is to invite derision, to reveal herself as one who does
not understand the sophisticated strategies of high culture and takes
art "too literally," and is therefore unable to respond to aesthetic

discourses. This is of course maintained within a world—a cultural and academic world—which is dominated by male power and, often unconscious, patriarchal attitudes. In Utopia—that is to say, in a world in which the power structure was such that both men and women equally could be represented clothed or unclothed in a variety of poses and positions without any implications of domination or submission—in a world of total and, so to speak, unconscious equality, the female nude would not be problematic. In our world, it is. As Laura Mulvey has pointed out in her often-cited article "Visual Pleasure and Narrative Cinema," there are two choices open to the woman spectator: either to take the place of the male or to accept the position of male-created seductive passivity and the questionable pleasure of masochism—lack of power to the nth degree.[37] This positioning of course offers an analogue to the actual status of women in the power structure of the art world—with the exception of the privileged few. To turn from the world of theory to that of mundane experience: I was participating as a guest in a college class on contemporary realism, when my host flashed on the screen the close-up image of a woman's buttocks in a striped bikini, as a presumed illustration of the substitution of part for whole in realist imagery, or perhaps it was the decorative impulse in realism. I commented on the overtly sexual—and sexist—implications of the image and the way it was treated. My host maintained that he "hadn't thought of that" and that he "had simply not been aware of the subject." It was impossible for any woman in the class "not to think of that" or for any man in the class to miss its crudely degrading implications. In a university art class, one is not supposed to speak of such things; women, like men, are presumably to take crudely fetishized motifs as signifiers of a refreshing liberatedness about sexual—and artistic—matters. My host insisted on the purely decorative, almost abstract, as he termed it, implications of the theme. But such abstraction is by no means a neutral strategy, as Daumier discovered when he transformed the recognizable head of Louis-Philippe into a neutral still-life object in his "La Poire" series. For women, the sexual positioning of the female in visual representation obtrudes through the apparently neutral or aesthetic fabric of the art work. Yet how little women protest, and

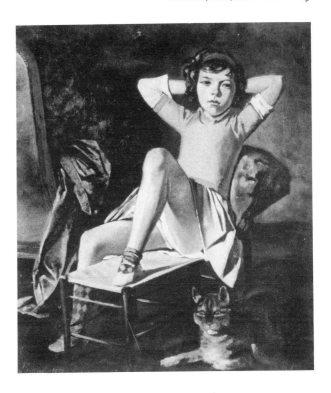

18. Balthus. *Girl with Cat (Thérèse Blanchard)*

with good reason, for, on the whole, they are in similarly powerless or marginalized positions within the operational structure of the art world itself: patient cataloguers rather than directors of museums; graduate students or junior faculty members rather than tenured professors and heads of departments; passive consumers rather than active creators of the art that is shown at major exhibitions.

A striking case in point was the dilemma of the female spectator at the Balthus exhibition which took place at the Metropolitan Museum of Art in New York in 1984.[38] A barrage of verbiage was directed at her to convince her that this was indeed great art; that to take too much notice of the perversity of the subject matter was not to "respond" to these masterpieces with the aesthetic distance they deserved; and that to protest on the grounds that these rep-

resentations of young women were disturbing was simply to respond to a major element in the grandeur of the artist's conception:
after all, they were "supposed to be" disturbing. To believe that
being disturbed by the representation of young women in sexually
perverse and provocative situations is a suitable object for questioning, much less for a negative critique, is considered the equivalent
of disapproval of the erotic itself [18]. But of course, women are
entitled to ask: "For whom, precisely, does this constitute an erotic
discourse? Why must I submit to a male-controlled discourse of the
erotic? In what sense is the gaze of the male fetishist equivalent to
and identical with an erotic discourse? Why must I accept a discourse that consistently mystifies my sexuality by constituting the
image of the vulnerable and seductive adolescent as a universally
erotic one?" And to those who hold up Balthus's canvases as more
general, radical images of transgression, one might well point out
that in terms of their language, they are scarcely transgressive at all,
extremely conservative, in fact, in the way they cling to an outmoded but modish language of visual repleteness, refusing to question the means of art except as the occasion of an added *frisson.* For
the daring deconstruction and questioning of patriarchal authority
central to Dada and to some aspects of Surrealism, Balthus's paintings substitute an unproblematically naturalistic replication of that
order; Balthus's oeuvre is, in fact, a prime exemplar of the *retour à
l'ordre* itself.

There is an analogy between women's compromised ability—
her lack of self-determining power—in the realm of the social order
and her lack of power to articulate a negative critique in the realm
of pictorial representation. In both cases, her rejection of patriarchal
authority is weakened by accusations of prudery or naïveté. Sophistication, liberation, belonging are equated with acquiescence to male
demands; women's initial perceptions of oppression, of outrage, of
negativity are undermined by authorized doubts, by the need to
please, to be learned, sophisticated, aesthetically astute—in male-
defined terms, of course. And the need to comply, to be inwardly
at one with the patriarchal order and its discourses is compelling,
inscribing itself in the deepest level of the unconscious, marking the
very definitions of the self-as-woman in our society—and almost all

others that we know of. I say this despite—indeed, because of—the obvious manifestations of change in the realm of women's power, position, and political consciousness brought about by the women's movement and more specifically by feminist criticism and art production over the last fifteen years. It is only by breaking the circuits, splitting apart those processes of harmonizing coherence that, to borrow the words of Lisa Tickner, "help secure the subject to and in ideology,"[39] by fishing in those invisible streams of power and working to demystify the discourses of visual imagery—in other words, through a politics of representation and its institutional structures—that change can take place.

Notes

1. For the most recent information about the three paintings usually referred to as *Past and Present*, see Lynda Nead, *Myths of Sexuality: Representations of Women in Victorian Britain* (London: Basil Blackwell, 1988), pp. 71–86.

2. Michel Foucault, *The History of Sexuality. Volume I: An Introduction* (New York: Pantheon, 1978), p. 86.

3. Robert Rosenblum has pointed out that David's theme may well have been the artist's own invention. See *Transformations in Late Eighteenth Century Art* (Princeton, N.J.: Princeton University Press, 1967), p. 68 and n. 68, pp. 68–69.

4. For a reproduction of Caraffe's *Oath of the Horatii* of 1791 (Arkangelski Castle), see the exhibition catalogue *French Painting, 1774–1830: The Age of Revolution*, Grand Palais, Paris, 1974–75; Detroit Institute of Arts, 1975; Metropolitan Museum of Art, New York, 1975, No. 18, p. 125.

5. For information about the change, see M. H. Noel-Patton, *Tales of a Granddaughter* (Elgin, Moray, Scotland: Moravian Press, 1970), p. 22.

6. See *Art Journal*, new series, IV (1858): 169, for a review of *In Memoriam*. The painting was No. 471 in the Royal Academy catalogue of that year.

7. For a full account of the daily life of British women in India in the nineteenth century, including their behavior during the Indian mutiny, see Pat Barr, *The Memsahibs: The Women of Victorian India* (London: Secker and Warburg, 1976).

8. The Spanish title of Goya's print is *Y son fieras*.

9. The photograph is taken from Midge Mackenzie, ed., *Shoulder to Shoulder: A Documentary* (New York: Knopf, 1st American ed., 1975), p. 255. It represents Mrs. Barrud, a well-known suffragette, demonstrating the methods of jujitsu.

10. Talcott Parsons, *Politics and Social Structure* (New York: Free Press, 1969), pp. 365–66. Parsons has observed: "The threat of coercive measures, or of compulsion, without legitimation or justification, should not properly be called the use of power at all, but is the limiting case where power, losing its symbolic character, merges into an intrinsic instrumentality of securing wishes, rather than obligations." Talcott Parsons, "On the Concept of Political Power," in *Sociological Theory and Modern*

Society (New York: Free Press, 1967), p. 331. Parsons's whole chapter, originally published in 1963, is relevant to a discussion of women and power, as is the preceding chapter in the same book, "Reflections on the Place of Force in Social Process" (pp. 264–96). See, for instance, Parsons's distinction between force and power: "In the context of deterrence, we conceive force to be a residual means that, in a showdown, is more effective than any alternative. Power, on the other hand, we conceive to be a *generalized* *medium* for controlling action—one among others— the effectiveness of which is dependent on a variety of factors of which control of force is only one, although a strategic one in *certain* contexts" (pp. 272–73).

11. This summary of Parsons's position is to be found in Arthur Kroker and David Cook, "Parsons' Foucault," in *The Postmodern Scene: Excremental Culture and Hyper-Aesthetics* (New York: St. Martin's Press, 1986), p. 228.

12. *Art Journal*, new series, IV (1858): 169.

13. "In Dreams Begin Responsibilities" is the title story of a book by the American poet Delmore Schwartz, published in 1938. Schwartz indicated that the title derived from an epigraph, "In dreams begins responsibility," which William Butler Yeats placed before his own collection *Responsibilities* (1914) and attributed to an "old play." Richard McDougall, *Delmore Schwartz* (New York: Twayne, 1974), pp. 46–47.

14. For the almost totally negative reception of Delacroix's painting, see Jack Spector, *Delacroix: The Death of Sardanapalus* (Art in Context) (New York: Viking, 1974), pp. 80–83.

15. Edward Said's *Orientalism* (New York: Pantheon Books, 1978) is the basic text on the subject of the representation of the Near East. Also see my article "The Imaginary Orient," *Art in America* 71 (May 1983): 118–131, upon which much of my analysis of Gérôme is based.

16. For a more detailed examination of the issues surrounding *The Ball at the Opera*, see my "A Thoroughly Modern Masked Ball," *Art in America* 71 (November 1983): 188–201.

17. Julius Meier-Graefe, *Édouard Manet* (Munich, 1912), p. 216. It must be understood that *The Ball at the Opera*, like so many Impressionist representations of so-called scenes of "leisure" or "entertainment," may actually be read as a kind of work scene: a representation of women in the entertainment or urban service industries. Bourgeois men's leisure was, and often still is, maintained or sustained by women's work, often work related to the marketing of their own bodies. *The Ball at the Opera*, like a Degas ballet scene or Manet's representations of café waitresses or prostitutes, is a representation of women's labor just as much as Millet's imagery of the female farmworker or domestic laborer. For some of the ambiguities surrounding the notion of prostitution as "work" in the nineteenth century, see T. J. Clark, *The Painting of Modern Life: Paris in the Art of Manet and His Followers* (New York: Knopf, 1985), pp. 101–8; Hollis Clayson, "*Avant-Garde* and *Pompier* Images of 19th Century French Prostitution: The Matter of Modernism, Modernity and Social Ideology," in Benjamin H. D. Buchloh, Serge Guilbaut, and David Solkin, eds., *Modernism and Modernity; The Vancouver Conference Papers*, Nova Scotia, Nova Scotia College of Art and Design, 1983, pp. 43–64; and Lynda Nead, *Myths of Sexuality: Representations of Women in Victorian Britain*, passim. For a variety of reasons, women's work both in the home and in the "entertainment" or "prostitution" trades escaped the Marxist analysis of production in the nineteenth century. See Linda Nicholson, "Feminism and Marx: Integrating Kinship with the

Economic," in *Feminism as Critique: On the Politics of Gender*, ed. S. Benhabib and
D. Cornell (Minneapolis, 1987), pp. 16–30.

18. For Mallarmé's view of the *Ball*, see his "Le Jury de peinture pour 1874 et M.
Manet," *Oeuvres complètes*, ed. H. Mondor and G. Jean-Aubry (Paris, 1945), p. 695.
The article originally appeared in *La Renaissance artistique et littéraire* in 1874. For
Mallarmé's comments on Manet's formal innovations see "The Impressionists and
Edouard Manet," an article which originally appeared in the 30 September 1876 issue
of *The Art Monthly Review and Photographic Portfolio* in London, and was recently
republished in the exhibition catalogue *The New Painting: Impressionism, 1874–1866*,
Fine Arts Museums of San Francisco and the National Gallery of Art, Washington,
D.C., 1986.

19. The trope of the fragmented legs in the medieval imagery of the ascending
Christ is discussed by Meyer Schapiro in "The Image of the Disappearing Christ:
The Ascension in English Art Around the Year 1000," *Gazette des Beaux-Arts*,
March 1943, pp. 135–52.

20. Stuart MacDonald, *The History and Philosophy of Art Education* (London:
University of London Press, 1970), title to Fig. 9, opp. p. 96. For the most recent
information on Emily Mary Osborn, see Charlotte Yeldham, *Women Artists in
Nineteenth-Century France and England* (New York and London: Garland, 1984),
vol. 1, p. 167, and pp. 309–11.

21. This is the interpretation of the painting given in the *Art Journal* of 1857, the
year when *Nameless and Friendless* was exhibited as No. 299 at the Royal Academy
Exhibition: "A poor girl has painted a picture, which she offers for sale to a dealer,
who, from the speaking expression of his features, is disposed to depreciate the
work. It is a wet, dismal day, and she has walked far to dispose of it; and now
awaits in trembling the decision of a man who is become rich by the labours of
others." *The Art Journal*, new series, III (1857): 170.

22. For a lengthy analysis of the representation of the peasant woman in
nineteenth-century, mostly French, art, see Linda Nochlin, "The *Cribleuses de blé:*
Courbet, Millet, Breton, Kollwitz and the Image of the Working Woman," in
Malerei und Theorie: Das Courbet-Colloquium 1979, ed. Klaus Gallwitz and Klaus
Herding, Frankfurt-am-Main, Städtische Galerie im Städelschen Kunstinstitut, 1980,
pp. 49–74.

23. See Paul de Grully, "Le Droit de glanage: Patrimonie des pauvres," Ph.D, Law
Faculty, University of Montpellier, 1912, for a complete historical examination of the
issue of gleaning.

24. For the most penetrating examination of the social contradictions embodied in
Millet's *Gleaners*, see Jean-Claude Chamboredon, "Peintures des rapports sociaux et
invention de l'éternel paysan: Les deux manières de Jean-François Millet," *Actes de
la recherche et sciences sociales*, nos. 17–18 (November 1977): 6–28.

25. I owe this observation to Robert Herbert.

26. See the exhibition catalogue *Käthe Kollwitz*, Frankfurter Kunstverein, 2nd ed.,
Frankfurt, 1973, Fig. 17.

27. Françoise Forster-Hahn, *Kaethe Kollwitz, 1867–1945: Prints, Drawings, Sculpture*,
exhibition catalogue, Riverside, California, University Art Galleries, 1978, p. 6.

28. Otto Nagel, *Kaethe Kollwitz*, trans. by S. Humphries (Greenwich, Conn.: New
York Graphic Society, 1971), p. 35.

29. Natalie Zemon Davis, "Woman on Top," in *Society and Culture in Early Modern France* (Stanford, Calif.: Stanford University Press, 1975), pp. 124–51 and especially p. 129.

30. "V'la une femme . . ." is part of the series "Les Divorceuses" and appeared in *Le Charivari* on August 12, 1848. The feminist to the left is meant to represent Eugénie Niboyet, who started the "Club des femmes" and the journal *La Voix des femmes*, which she holds with the title partly hidden behind her back. The figure to the right is probably meant to refer to Jeanne Deroin, a feminist activist who was frequently the butt of Daumier's scathing satire in his anti-feminist series "Les Femmes Socialistes," which appeared in *Le Charivari* from April to June 1849. See Jan Rie Kist, *Honoré Daumier, 1808–1879*, exhibition catalogue, National Gallery of Art, Washington, D.C., 1979, No. 58, p. 59, and Françoise Parturier, *Intellectuelles (Bas Bleus et Femmes Socialistes)* (Paris: Éditions Vilo-Paris, 1974), passim. For a study of Daumier's anti-feminist caricatures, see Caecillia Rentmeister, "Daumier und das hässliche Geschlecht," in the exhibition catalogue *Daumier und die ungelösten Probleme der bürgerlichen Gesellschaft* (Berlin: Schloss Charlottenburg, 1974), pp. 57–79.

31. For a discussion of caricatures of women of the Commune, see James A. Leith, *Images of the Commune* (Montreal and London, 1978), pp. 135–38, and Adrian Rifkin, "No Particular Thing to Mean," *Block* 8 (1983): 36–45.

32. Natalie Zemon Davis, *Society and Culture in Early Modern Europe*, p. 129.

33. This frightening aspect of Black Anna is manifested particularly in the print from the series entitled "Whetting the Scythe," a soft-ground etching, in which the figure looms out at the spectator from a shadowy background, her weapon clutched to her body, her expression a kind of brooding malevolence.

34. Midge Mackenzie, ed., *Shoulder to Shoulder*, pp. 258–61. Also see Lisa Tickner, *The Spectacle of Women: Imagery of the Suffrage Campaign, 1907–14* (Chicago: University of Chicago Press, 1988), p. 134.

35. Jacqueline Rose, "Sexuality in the Field of Vision," in *Sexuality in the Field of Vision* (London: Verso, 1986), p. 232.

36. Peter Wollen, "Counter-Cinema and Sexual Difference," in *Difference: On Representation and Sexuality*, exhibition catalogue, New York, New Museum of Contemporary Art, 1985.

37. Laura Mulvey, "Visual Pleasure and Narrative Cinema," *Screen* 16, no. 3 (Autumn 1975): 6–18. As Mulvey herself has later pointed out, this is perhaps too simple a conception of the possibilities involved. Nevertheless, it still seems to offer a good working conception for beginning to think about the position of the female spectator of the visual arts.

38. See the exhibition catalogue *Balthus*, by Sabine Rewald, New York, Metropolitan Museum of Art and Harry N. Abrams, 1984.

39. Lisa Tickner, "Sexuality and/in Representation: Five British Artists," in *Difference: On Representation and Sexuality*, p. 20.

2

Morisot's *Wet Nurse:*
The Construction of Work and
Leisure in Impressionist Painting

Tant de clairs tableaux irisés, ici, exacts, primesautiers. . . .
Stéphane Mallarmé[1]

Berthe Morisot's *Wet Nurse and Julie* [1] of 1879 is an extraordinary painting.[2] Even in the context of an oeuvre in which formal daring is relatively unexceptional, this work is outstanding. "All that is solid melts into air"—Karl Marx's memorable phrase, made under rather different circumstances, could have been designed for the purpose of encapsulating Morisot's painting in a nutshell.[3] Nothing is left of the conventions of pictorial construction: figure versus background, solid form versus atmosphere, detailed description versus sketchy suggestion, the usual complexities of composition or narration. All are abandoned for a composition almost disconcerting in its three-part simplicity; a facture so open, so dazzlingly unfettered as to constitute a challenge to readability; and a colorism so daring, so synoptic in its rejection of traditional strategies of modeling as to be almost Fauve before the fact.[4]

Morisot's *Wet Nurse* is equally innovative in its subject matter. For this is not the old motif of the Madonna and Child, updated and secularized, as it is in a work like Renoir's *Aline Nursing* or in many of the mother-and-child paintings by the other prominent woman member of the Impressionist group, Mary Cassatt. It is, surprisingly enough, a work scene. The "mother" in the scene is not a real

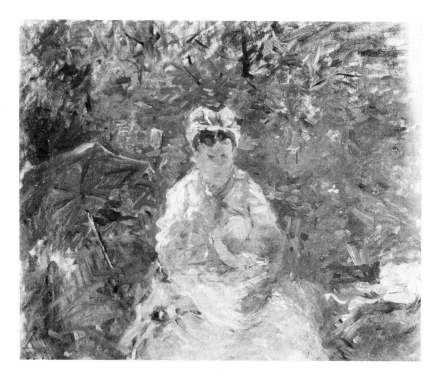

1. Berthe Morisot. *Wet Nurse and Julie*

mother but a so-called *seconde mère,* or wet nurse, and she is feeding
the child not out of "natural" nurturing instinct but for wages, as
a member of a flourishing industry.[5] And the artist painting her,
whose gaze defines her, whose active brush articulates her form, is
not, as is usually the case, a man, but a woman, the woman whose
child is being nursed. Certainly, this painting embodies one of the
most unusual circumstances in the history of art—perhaps a unique
one: a woman painting another woman nursing her baby. Or, to put
it another way, introducing what is not seen but what is known into
what is visible, two working women confront each other here,
across the body of "their" child and the boundaries of class, both
with claims to motherhood and mothering, both, one assumes, engaged in pleasurable activity which, at the same time, may be considered production in the literal sense of the word. What might be
considered a mere use value if the painting was produced by a mere

amateur, the milk produced for the nourishment of one's own child, is now to be understood as an exchange value. In both cases—the milk, the painting—a product is being produced or created for a market, for profit.

Once we know this, when we look at the picture again we may find that the openness, the disembodiment, the reduction of the figures of nurser and nursling almost to caricature, to synoptic adumbration, may be the signs of erasure, of tension, of the conscious or unconscious occlusion of a painful and disturbing reality as well as the signs of daring and pleasure—or perhaps these signs, under the circumstances, may be identical, inseparable from each other. One might say that this representation of the classical topos of the maternal body poignantly inscribes Morisot's conflicted identity as devoted mother and as professional artist, two roles which, in nineteenth-century discourse, were defined as mutually exclusive. *The Wet Nurse*, then, turns out to be much more complicated than it seemed to be at first, and its stimulating ambiguities may have as much to do with the contradictions involved in contemporary mythologies of work and leisure, and the way that ideologies of gender intersect with these paired notions, as they do with Morisot's personal feelings and attitudes.

Reading *The Wet Nurse* as a work scene inevitably leads me to locate it within the representation of the thematics of work in nineteenth-century painting, particularly that of the woman worker. It also raises the issue of the status of work as a motif in Impressionist painting—its presence or absence as a viable theme for the group of artists which counted Morisot as an active member. And I will also want to examine the particular profession of wet-nursing itself as it relates to the subject of Morisot's canvas.

How was work positioned in the advanced art of the later nineteenth century, at the time when Morisot painted this picture? Generally in the art of this period, work, as Robert Herbert has noted,[6] was represented by the rural laborer, usually the male peasant engaged in productive labor on the farm. This iconography reflected a certain statistical truth, since most of the working population of France at the time was, in fact, engaged in farm work. Although representations of the male farm worker predominated, this is not to say that the female rural laborer was absent from French painting of the second half of the nineteenth century. Millet often represented peasant women at work at domestic tasks like spinning or churning, and Jules Breton specialized in scenes of idealized peasant women working in the fields. But it is nevertheless significant that in the quintessential representation of the labor of the female peasant, Millet's *Gleaners*, women are represented engaged not in productive labor—that is, working for profit, for the market—but rather for sheer personal survival—that is, for the nurturance of themselves and their children, picking up what is left over after the productive labor of the harvest is finished.[7] The *glaneuses* are thus assimilated to the realm of the natural—rather like animals that forage to feed themselves and their young—rather than to that of the social, to the realm of productive labor. This assimilation of the peasant woman to the position of the natural and the nurturant is made startlingly clear in a painting like Giovanni Segantini's *Two Mothers* [2], which makes a visual analogy between cow and woman as instinctive nurturers of their young.

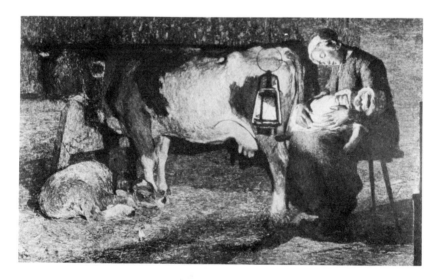

2. Giovanni Segantini. *The Two Mothers*, detail

Work occupies an ambiguous position in the representational systems of Impressionism, the movement to which Morisot was irrevocably connected; or one might say that acknowledgment of the presence of work themes in Impressionism has until recently been repressed in favor of discourses stressing the movement's "engagement with themes of urban leisure."[8] Meyer Schapiro, above all, in two important articles of the 1930s, laid down the basic notion of Impressionism as a representation of middle-class leisure, sociability, and recreation depicted from the viewpoint of the enlightened, sensually alert middle-class consumer.[9] One could contravene this contention by pointing to a body of Impressionist works that do, in fact, continue the tradition of representing rural labor initiated in the previous generation by Courbet and Millet and popularized in more sentimental form by Breton and Bastien-Lepage. Pissarro, particularly, continued to develop the motif of the peasant, particularly the laboring or resting peasant woman, and that of the market woman in both Impressionist and Neo-Impressionist vocabularies, right down through the 1880s. Berthe Morisot herself turned to the theme of rural labor several times: once in *The Haymaker,* a beautiful preparatory drawing for a larger decorative composition; again, in a little painting, *In the Wheat Field,* of 1875; and still another time (more ambiguously, because the rural "workers" in question, far from being peasants, are her daughter, Julie, and her niece Jeanne picking cherries) in *The Cherry Tree* of 1891–92.[10] Certainly, one could point to a significant body of Impressionist work representing urban or suburban labor. Degas did a whole series of ironers;[11] Caillebotte depicted floor scrapers and house painters; and Morisot herself turned at least twice to the theme of the laundress: once in *Laundresses Hanging out the Wash* of 1875, a lyrical canvas of commercial laundresses plying their trade in the environs of the city, painted with a synoptic lightness that seems to belie the laboriousness of the theme; and another time in *Woman Hanging the Washing* [3], of 1881, a close-up view where the rectangularity of the linens seems wittily to reiterate the shape and texture of the canvas, the laundress to suggest the work of the woman artist herself. Clearly, then, the Impressionists by no means totally avoided the representation of work.

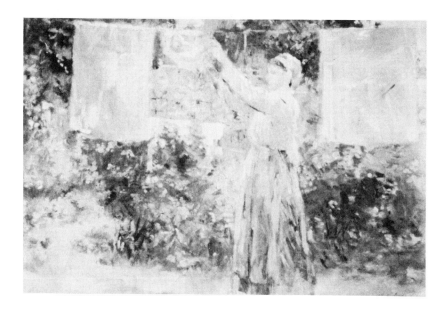

3. Berthe Morisot. *Woman Hanging the Washing*

    To speak more generally, however, interpreting Impressionism as a movement constituted primarily by the representation of leisure has to do as much with a particular characterization of labor as with the iconography of the Impressionist movement. In the ideological constructions of the French Third Republic, as I have already pointed out, work was epitomized by the notion of rural labor, in the time-honored, physically demanding, naturally ordained tasks of peasants on the land. The equally demanding physical effort of ballet dancing, represented by Degas, with its hours of practice, its strains, its endless repetition and sweat, was constructed as something else, something different: as art or entertainment. Of course this construction has something to do with the way entertainment represents itself: often the whole point of the work of dancing is to make it look as though it is not work, that it is spontaneous and easy.

    But there is a still more interesting general point to be made about Impressionism and its reputed affinity with themes of leisure and pleasure. It is the tendency to conflate *woman's* work—whether it be her work in the service or entertainment industries or, above all, her work in the home—with the notion of leisure itself. As a result, our notion of the iconography of work, framed as it is by the stereotype of the peasant in the fields or the weaver at his loom, tends to exclude such subjects as the barmaid or the beer server from the category of the work scene and position them instead as representations of leisure. One might even say, looking at such paintings as Manet's *Bar at the Folies-Bergère* or his *Beer Server* from the vantage point of the new women's history, that middle- and upper-class men's leisure is sustained and enlivened by the labor of women: entertainment and service workers like those represented by Manet.[12] It is also clear that these representations position women workers—barmaid or beer server—in such a way that they seem to be there to be looked at—visually consumed, as it were—by a male viewer. In the *Beer Server* of 1878, for example, the busy waitress looks out alertly at the clientele, while the relaxed male in the foreground—ironically a worker himself, identifiable by his blue smock—stares placidly at the woman performer, half visible, doing her act on the stage. The work of café waitresses or performers, like those represented by Degas in his pastels of café concerts, is often connected to their sexuality or, more specifically, the sex industry of the time, whether marginally or centrally, full time or part time. What women, specifically lower-class women, had to sell in the city was mainly their bodies. A comparison of Manet's *Ball at the Opera* —denominated by the German critic Julius Meier-Graefe as a *Fleischebörse,* or flesh market—with Degas's *Cotton Market in New Orleans* makes it clear that work, rather than being an objective or logical category, is an evaluative or even a moral one. Men's leisure is produced and maintained by women's work, disguised to look like pleasure. The concept of work under the French Third Republic was constructed in terms of what that society or its leaders stipulated as good, productive activity, generally conceived of as wage-earning or capital production. Women's selling of their bodies for wages did not fall under the moral rubric of work; it was constructed as something else: as vice or recreation. Prostitutes (ironically, referred to colloquially as "working girls" today), a subject often represented by Degas, like the businessmen represented in his *Members of the*

Stock Exchange, are of course engaging in a type of commercial activity. But nobody has ever thought to call the prints from Degas's monotype series of brothel representations "work scenes," despite the fact that prostitutes, like wet nurses and barmaids and laundresses, were an important part of the work force of the great modern city in the nineteenth century, and in Paris, at this time, a highly regulated, government-supervised form of labor.[13]

If prostitution was excluded from the realm of honest work because it involved women selling their bodies, motherhood and the domestic labor of child care were excluded from the realm of work precisely because they were unpaid. Woman's nurturing role was seen as part of her natural function, not as labor. The wet nurse [4], then, is something of an anomaly in the nineteenth-century scheme of feminine labor. She is like the prostitute in that she sells her body, or its product, for profit and her client's satisfaction; but, unlike the prostitute, she sells her body for a virtuous cause. She is at once a mother—*seconde mère, remplaçant*—and an employee. She is per-

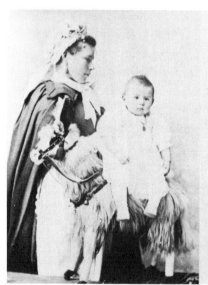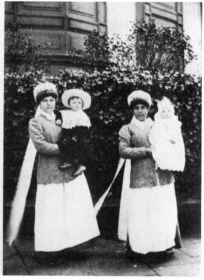

4. *Wet Nurses.* Anonymous French photographs from about 1900

forming one of woman's "natural" functions, but she is performing it as work, for pay, in a way that is eminently not natural but overtly social in its construction.

To understand Morisot's *Wet Nurse and Julie,* one has to locate the profession of wet-nursing within the context of nineteenth-century social and cultural history. Wet-nursing constituted a large-scale industry in France in the eighteenth and nineteenth centuries. In the nineteenth century, members of the urban artisan and shop-keeping classes usually sent their children out to be nursed by women in the country so that wives would be free to work. So large was the *industrie nourricière* and so patent the violations of sanitation, so high the mortality rate and so unsteady the financial arrangements involved that the government stepped in to regulate the industry in 1874 with the so-called Loi Roussel, which supervised wet nurses and their clients on a nationwide basis.[14] Members of the aristocracy or upper bourgeoisie such as Berthe Morisot, however, did not have to resort to this "regulated" industry. They usually hired a *nourrice sur lieu,* or live-in wet nurse, who accompanied the infant, took it to the park, and comforted it—but was there mainly to provide the baby with nourishment.[15] The omnipresence of the wet nurse in the more fashionable purlieus of Parisian society is indicated in Degas's *Carriage at the Races* [5], where the Valpinçons, husband and wife, are accompanied by their dog, by their son and heir, Henri, and by the veritable star of the piece, the wet nurse, depicted in the act of feeding the baby.[16] A foreign painter like the Finnish Albert Edelfelt, when depicting the charms of Parisian upper-class life, quite naturally included the wet nurse in his *Luxembourg Gardens,* a painting of 1887 now in the Antell Collection in Helsinki; and Georges Seurat incorporated the figure, severely geometrized, into the cross section of French society he represented in *A Sunday on the Island of La Grande-Jatte.*

The wet nurse was, on the one hand, considered the most "spoiled" servant in the house and, at the same time, the most closely watched and supervised. She was in some ways considered more like a highly prized milch cow than a human being. Although she was relatively highly paid for her services, often bringing home 1,200 to 1,800 francs per campaign—her salary ranked just under that of the

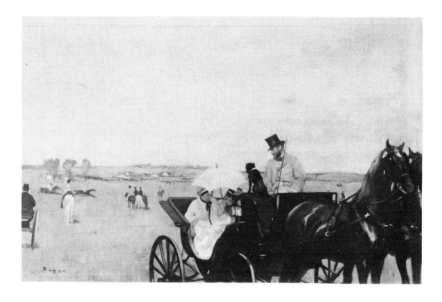

5. Edgar Degas. *Carriage at the Races*

cordon bleu chef[17]—and was often presented with clothing and other valuable gifts, her diet, though plentiful and choice, was carefully monitored and her sex life was brought to a halt; and of course, she had to leave her own baby at home in the care of her own mother or another family member.[18]

The wet nurse was always a country woman, and generally from a specific region of the country: the Morvan, for instance, was considered prime wet-nurse territory.[19] Wet-nursing was the way poor country women with few valuable skills could make a relatively large sum of money: selling their services to well-off urban families. The analogy with today's surrogate mothers makes itself felt immediately, except that the wet nurse was not really the subject of any moral discourse about exploitation; on the contrary: although some doctors and child-care specialists complained about the fact that natural mothers refused to take nature's way and breast-feed their children themselves, in general they preferred a healthy wet nurse to a nervous new mother. Few upper-class women in the later nineteenth century would have dreamed of breast-feeding their own children; and only a limited proportion of women of the artisan class, who had to work themselves or who lived in crowded quarters, had the chance to do so. If Renoir proudly represented his wife nursing their son Jean, it was not because it was so "natural" for her to do so, but perhaps because, on the contrary, it was not. Renoir's wife, in any case, was not of the same social class as Berthe Morisot; she was of working-class origin. Berthe Morisot, then, was being perfectly "natural" within the perimeters of her class in hiring a wet nurse. It would not be considered neglectful and certainly would not have to be excused by the fact that she was a serious professional painter: it was simply what people of her social station did.

The wet nurse, in various aspects of her career, was frequently represented in popular visual culture, and her image appeared often in the press or in genre paintings dealing with the typical trades or professions of the capital. A forgotten painter of the later nineteenth century, José de Frappa, in his *Bureau de Nourrice* depicted the medical examination of potential wet nurses in an employment bureau. Husband, mother-in-law, and doctor evidently participated in the choice of a candidate. Wet-nursing was frequently the subject of humorous caricatures right down to the beginning of the twentieth century, when sterilization and pasteurization enabled mothers to substitute the newly hygienic bottle for the human breast—and thereby gave rise to cartoons dealing with the wet nurse attempting to compete with her replacement.[20] With her ruffled, beribboned cap and jacket or cape, she was frequently depicted in illustrations of fashionable parks, where she aired her charges, or in those of upper-class households. Her characteristic form could even serve to illustrate the letter *N*—for *nourrice*—in a children's alphabet [6]. Degas, like Seurat, was evidently struck by the typical back view of this familiar figure and sketched it in one of his notebooks [7].

Morisot is not, of course, in her paintings of her daughter and her wet nurse[21] creating a sociological document of a particular kind of work or even a genre scene of some engaging incident involved in wet-nursing. Both Julie and her wet nurse serve as motifs in highly original Impressionist paintings, and their specificity as documents of social practice is hardly of conscious interest to the creator of the paintings, who is intent on creating an equivalent for

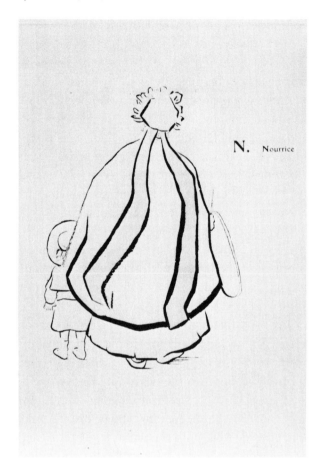

N.   Nourrice

6. *Letter "N": Nourrice.* Illustration from children's
alphabet

her perceptions through visual qualities of color, brushwork, light,
shape—or the deconstruction of shape—and atmosphere. Nor do
we think of Morisot as primarily a painter of work scenes; she was,
indeed, one of those artists of the later nineteenth century—like
Whistler and Manet, among others—who helped construct a specific iconography of leisure, figured by young and attractive
women, whose role was simply to be there, for the painter, as a
languid and self-absorbed object of aesthetic contemplation—a kind

of human still life. Her *Portrait of Mme Marie Hubbard* of 1874 and *Young Girl Reclining* of 1893 are notable examples of this genre. Morisot is associated, quite naturally, not with work scenes, however ambiguous, but rather with the representation of domestic life, mothers, or, more rarely, fathers—specifically her husband, Eugène Manet—and daughters engaged in recreation [8]. This father-and-daughter motif is, like the theme of the wet nurse, an unusual one in the annals of Impressionist painting. Male Impressionists who,

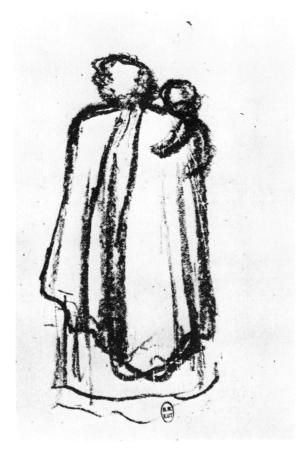

7. Edgar Degas. *Drawing of Wet Nurse from the Rear*

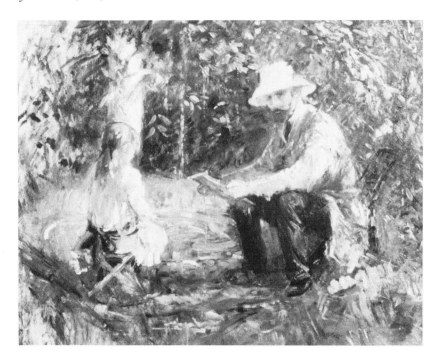

8. Berthe Morisot. *Eugène Manet and His Daughter in the Garden*

like Morisot, turned to the domestic world around them for subject matter, painted their wives and children as a matter of course. Here is a case where being a woman artist makes an overt difference: Morisot, in turning to her closest relatives, paints a father and child, a rather unusual theme in the annals of Impressionism, and one with its own kinds of demands. She depicts her husband and daughter doing something concrete—playing with a boat and sketching or playing with toy houses—and with a vaguely masculine air.

Despite the fact that scenes of leisure, languor, and recreation are prominent in Morisot's oeuvre, there is another way we might think of work in relation to her production. The notion of the work of painting itself is never disconnected from her art and is perhaps allegorized in various toilette scenes in which women's self-preparation and adornment stand for the art of painting or subtly refer to it.[22] A simultaneous process of looking and creating are prime elements of a woman's toilette as well as picture-making, and sensual pleasure as well as considerable effort is involved in both. One could even go further and assert that in both—maquillage and painting—a private creation is being prepared for public approbation.

Painting was work of the utmost seriousness for Morisot. She was, as the recent exhibition catalogue of her work reveals to us,[23] unsparing of herself, perpetually dissatisfied, often destroying works or groups of works that did not satisfy her high standards. Her mother observed that whenever she worked, she had an "anxious, unhappy, almost fierce look," adding, "This existence of hers is like the ordeal of a convict in chains."[24]

There is another sense in which Morisot's oeuvre may be associated with the work of painting: the way in which the paintings reveal the act of working which creates them, are sparkling, invigorating, and totally uneffortful-looking registers of the process of painting itself. In the best of them, color and brushstroke are the deliberately revealed point of the picture: they are, so to speak, works about work, in which the work of looking and registering the process of looking in paint on canvas or pastel on paper assumes an importance almost unparalleled in the annals of painting. One might almost say that the work of painting is not so strongly revealed until the time of the late Monet or even that of Abstract Expressionism, although for the latter, of course, looking and registering were not the issue.[25]

Even when Morisot looked at herself, as in her 1885 *Self-Portrait with Julie,* boldly, on unprimed canvas, or in her pastel *Self-Portrait* of the same year, the work of painting or marking was primary: these are in no sense flattering or even conventionally penetrating self-portraits: they are, especially the pastel version, working records of an appearance, deliberate in their telling asymmetries, their revelation of brushwork or marking, unusual above all for their omissions, their selective recording of a motif that happens to be the author's face. The pastel *Self-Portrait* is almost painfully moving. It is no wonder that critics sometimes found her work too sketchy, unfinished, bold to the point of indecipherability. Referring to two of her pastels, for example, Charles Ephrussi declared: "One step

further and it will be impossible to distinguish or understand anything at all."[26]

In her late *Girl with a Greyhound* [9], a portrait of Julie with a
dog and an empty chair, painted in 1893, Morisot dissolves the chair
into a vision of evanescent lightness: a work of omission, of almost
nothingness. Compared with it, van Gogh's famous *Gauguin's Chair*
looks heavy, solid, and a little overwrought. Yet Morisot's chair is
moving, too. Its ghostliness and disembodiment remind us that it
was painted shortly after her husband's death, perhaps as an emblem
of his absent presence within the space of his daughter's portrait.
And perhaps for us, who know that she painted this at the end of
her life, it may constitute a moving yet self-effacing prophecy of her
own impending death, an almost unconscious means of establishing

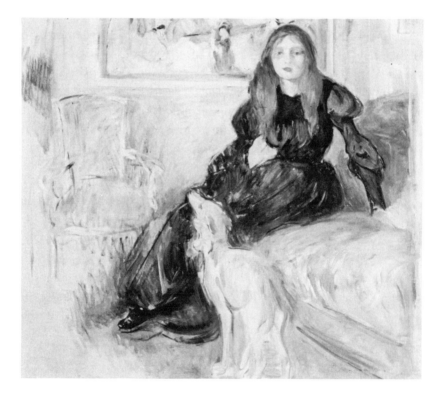

9. Berthe Morisot. *Girl with a Greyhound (Julie Manet)*

—lightly, only in terms of the work itself—her presence within an image representing, for the last time, her beloved only child.

In insisting on the importance of work, specifically the traces of manual activity, in Morisot's production, I am not suggesting that Morisot's work was the same as the onerous physical labor involved in farm work or the routine mechanical efforts of the factory hand —nor that it was identical with the relatively mindless and constricted duties of the wet nurse. We can, however, see certain connections: in a consideration of both the work of the wet nurse and that of the woman artist the element of gender asserts itself. Most critics both then and now have emphasized Morisot's gender; her femininity was constructed from an essentialist viewpoint as delicacy, instinctiveness, naturalness, playfulness—a construction implying certain natural gendered lacks or failures: lack of depth, of substance, professionalism or leadership, for instance. Why else has Morisot always been considered as somehow a secondary Impressionist, despite her exemplary fidelity to the movement and its aims? Why has her very flouting of the traditional "laws" of painting been seen as a weakness rather than a strength, a failure or lack of knowledge and ability rather than a daring transgression? Why should the disintegration of form characteristic of her best work not be considered a vital questioning of Impressionism from within, a "making strange" of its more conventional practices? And if we consider that erosion of form to be a complexly mediated inscription of internalized conflict—motherhood versus profession—then surely this should be taken as seriously as the more highly acclaimed psychic dramas of male artists of the period: van Gogh's struggle with his madness; Cézanne's with a turbulent sexuality; Gauguin's with the contering urgencies of sophistication and primitivism.

I would like to end as I began, with Karl Marx's memorable phrase: "All that is solid melts into air." But now I would like to consider the whole passage, from the *Communist Manifesto*, from which I (and Marshall Berman, author of a book titled by that passage) extracted it. Here is the whole passage: "All fixed, fast-frozen relations, with their train of ancient and venerable prejudices and opinions, are swept away, all new-formed ones become antiquated before they can ossify: All that is solid melts into air, all that is holy is profaned, and men at last are forced to face . . . the real conditions of their lives and their relations with their fellow men."[27]

I am not in any sense suggesting that Morisot was a political or even a social revolutionary—far from it. But I am saying that her strange, fluid, unclassifiable, and contradiction-laden image *Wet Nurse and Julie* inscribes many of those characteristic features of modernism and modernity that Marx is of course referring to in his celebrated passage—above all, modernism's profoundly deconstructive project. Sweeping away "all fixed and frozen relations with their accompanying prejudices and opinions"—this is certainly Morisot's project as well. And in some way too, she is in this picture, being forced to face, at the same time that it is impossible for her fully to face, the real condition of her life and her relations with a fellow woman. Thinking of Marx's words, looking at Morisot's painting, I sense these real conditions hovering on the surface of the canvas, a surface as yet not fully explored, untested but still potentially threatening to "ancient and venerable prejudices and opinions"—about the nature of work, about gender, and about painting itself.

Notes

1. Preface to the catalogue of the posthumous exhibition of Berthe Morisot's paintings, Durand-Ruel Gallery, Paris, March 5–23, 1896.

2. The painting was exhibited under the title *Nourrice et bébé* (Wet Nurse and Baby) at the Sixth Impressionist Exhibition of 1880. It is also known under the title *La Nourrice Angèle allaitant Julie Manet* (The Wet Nurse Angèle Feeding Julie Manet) and *Nursing*. See the exhibition catalogue *The New Painting: Impressionism, 1874–1886*, Fine Arts Museums of San Francisco and National Gallery of Art, Washington, D.C., 1986, No. 110, p. 366, and Charles F. Stuckey and William P. Scott, *Berthe Morisot: Impressionist*, exhibition catalogue, National Gallery of Art, Washington, D.C.; Kimbell Art Museum, Fort Worth, Texas; Mount Holyoke College Art Museum, 1987–88, Fig. 41, p. 89 and p. 88.

3. Karl Marx's statement may be found in Robert C. Tucker, ed., *The Marx-Engels Reader* (New York: Norton, 1978), p. 476.

4. The critic Gustave Geffroy responded to the *Wet Nurse*'s unique qualities when he reviewed Morisot's work from the Sixth Impressionist Exhibition in *La Justice* of April 21, 1881, by waxing lyrical: "The forms are always vague in Berthe Morisot's paintings, but a strange life animates them. The artist has found the means to fix the play of colors, the quivering between things and the air that envelops them. . . . Pink, pale green, faintly gilded light sings with an inexpressible harmony." Cited in *The New Painting: Impressionism, 1874–1886*, p. 366.

5. Indeed, one might suspect that the unusual sketchiness and rapidity of the brushwork may have had something to do with Morisot's haste to complete her painting within the course of a single nursing session. Nevertheless, she obviously did not consider the painting a mere preparatory study, since she exhibited it in public as a finished work.

6. Robert Herbert, "City vs. Country: The Rural Image in French Painting from Millet to Gauguin," *Artforum* 8 (February 1970): 44–55.

7. See Jean-Claude Chamboredon, "Peintures des rapports sociaux et invention de l'éternel paysan: Les deux manières de Jean-François Millet," *Actes de la recherche et sciences sociales*, Nos. 17–18 (November 1977): 6–28.

8. Thomas Crow, "Modernism and Mass Culture in the Visual Arts," in *Modernism and Modernity: The Vancouver Conference Papers*, ed. Benjamin H. D. Buchloh, Serge Guilbaut, and David Solkin, Nova Scotia, The Nova Scotia College of Art and Design, 1983, p. 226.

9. See Meyer Schapiro, "The Social Bases of Art," in *Proceedings of the First Artists' Congress against War and Fascism*, New York, 1936, pp. 31–37, and "The Nature of Abstract Art," *The Marxist Quarterly* I (January 1937): 77–98, reprinted in Schapiro, *Modern Art: The Nineteenth and Twentieth Centuries* (New York: George Braziller), especially pp. 192–93.

10. For an illustration of *The Haymaker*, see *Berthe Morisot: Impressionist*, Colorplate 93, p. 159; for *In the Wheatfield*, Kathleen Adler and Tamar Garb, *Berthe Morisot* (Ithaca, N.Y.: Cornell University Press, 1987), Fig. 89; and *The Cherry Tree*, *Berthe Morisot: Impressionist*, Colorplate 89, p. 153.

11. For a detailed discussion of Degas's ironers and laundresses, see Eunice Lipton, *Looking into Degas: Uneasy Images of Women and Modern Life* (Berkeley: University of California Press, 1986), pp. 116–50.

12. For the role of the barmaid in French nineteenth-century society and iconography, see T. J. Clark, *The Painting of Modern Life: Paris in the Art of Manet and His Followers* (Princeton, N.J.: Princeton University Press, 1984), pp. 205–58, and Novalene Ross, *Manet's "Bar at the Folies-Bergère" and the Myths of Popular Illustration* (Ann Arbor: University of Michigan Press, 1982).

13. For information about government regulation of prostitution, see Alain Corbin, *Les Filles de noce: Misère sexuelle et prostitution aux 19e et 20e siècles* (Paris, 1978); for the representation of prostitution in the art of the later nineteenth century, see Hollis Clayson, "*Avant-Garde* and *Pompier* Images of 19th Century French Prostitution: The Matter of Modernism, Modernity and Social Ideology," in *Modernism and Modernity*, pp. 43–64. Meier-Graefe uses the term "Fleischbörse" in *Édouard Manet* (Munich: Piper Verlag, 1912), p. 216.

14. For the Roussel Law of December 23, 1874, see George D. Sussman, *Selling Mothers' Milk: The Wet-Nursing Business in France: 1715–1914* (Urbana: University of Illinois Press, 1982), pp. 128–29 and 166–67.

15. For an excellent examination of the role of the wet nurse in the nineteenth century, focusing on the *nourrice sur lieu* and including an analysis of the medical discourse surrounding the issue of maternal breast-feeding, see Fanny Faÿ-Sallois, *Les Nourrices à Paris au XIXe siècle* (Paris: Payot, 1980).

16. I am grateful to Paul Tucker for pointing out the presence of the wet nurse in this painting.

17. Faÿ-Sallois, *Les Nourrices à Paris aux XIXe siècle*, p. 201.

18. For the figures of the wages cited, see Sussman, *Selling Mothers' Milk: The Wet-Nursing Business in France: 1715–1914*, p. 155, and for the salary of the live-in wet nurse and her treatment generally, see Faÿ-Sallois, *Les Nourrices à Paris aux XIXe siècle*, pp. 200–39.

19. Sussman, *Selling Mothers' Milk: The Wet-Nursing Business in France: 1715–1914*, pp. 152–54.

20. See, particularly, the vicious cartoon depicting a wet nurse attempting to boil her breast in emulation of bottle sterilization, published by Faÿ-Sallois, *Les Nourrices à Paris au XIXe siècle*, p. 247. Other interesting cartoons featuring wet-nursing and the practices associated with it appear on pp. 172–73, p. 188, and p. 249 of this work, which is amply illustrated.

21. There are at least two other works by Morisot representing her daughter, Julie, and her wet nurse: an oil painting, *Julie with Her Nurse*, 1880, now in the Ny Carlsberg Glyptotek, Copenhagen, reproduced as Fig. 68 in Adler and Garb, *Berthe Morisot;* and a watercolor entitled *Luncheon in the Country* of 1879, in which the wet nurse and baby are seated at a table with a young boy, probably Morisot's nephew Marcel Gobillard, reproduced as Colorplate 32, p. 77, in Stuckey and Scott, *Berthe Morisot: Impressionist.*

22. See, for example, *Woman at Her Toilette*, ca. 1879, in the Art Institute of Chicago or *Young Woman Powdering Her Face* of 1877, Paris, Musée d'Orsay.

23. Charles Stuckey and William Scott, *Berthe Morisot: Impressionist,* National Gallery of Art, Washington, D.C.; Kimbell Art Museum, Fort Worth, Texas; Mount Holyoke College Art Museum, 1987–88.

24. Stuckey and Scott, *Berthe Morisot: Impressionist,* p. 187.

25. See, for example, Charles Stuckey's assertion that, in the case of *Wet Nurse and Julie,* "it is difficult to think of a comparably active paint surface by any painter before the advent of Abstract Expressionism in the 1950s." *Berthe Morisot: Impressionist,* p. 88.

26. Cited in Stuckey and Scott, *Berthe Morisot: Impressionist,* p. 88.

27. Cited by Marshall Berman in *All That Is Solid Melts into Air: The Experience of Modernity* (New York: Simon and Schuster, 1982), p. 21.

3

Lost and *Found:*
Once More the Fallen Woman

———

"It's a queer thing," muses a young woman in one of Rose Macaulay's novels, written shortly after the First World War, "how 'fallen' in the masculine means killed in the war, and in the feminine given over to a particular kind of vice." The sexual asymmetry peculiar to the notion of falling is worth considering, especially in the nineteenth century, when both aspects were taken more seriously than they are today. In art, fallen in the masculine tended to inspire rather boring sculptural monuments and sarcophagi. Fallen in the feminine, however—understood as any sort of sexual activity on the part of women out of wedlock, whether or not for gain—exerted a peculiar fascination on the imagination of nineteenth-century artists, not to speak of writers, social critics, and uplifters, an interest that reached its peak in England in the middle years of the nineteenth century, and that perhaps received its characteristic formulation in the circle of the Pre-Raphaelites and their friends. Certainly the theme of the fallen woman may be said to have interested Dante Gabriel Rossetti almost to the point of obsession. Not only did he devote a number of poems and pictorial works to the subject, but his one painting to deal with a contemporary subject in an unaccustomed realistic mode was devoted to the theme. This painting,

———

Found [1], significantly unfinished, occupied him on and off from at least as early as 1853 until the year before his death: it was obviously a work he could never fully resolve or definitely put aside.[1]

Rossetti's description of the picture in a letter to Holman Hunt of 30 January 1855 seems straightforward enough:

> *The picture represents a London street at dawn, with the lamps*
> *still lighted along a bridge which forms the distant background.*
> *A drover has left his cart standing in the middle of the road (in*
> *which, i.e., the cart, stands baa-ing a calf tied on its way to*
> *market), and has run a little way after a girl who has passed*
> *him, wandering in the streets. He had just come up with her and*
> *she, recognizing him, has sunk under her shame upon her knees,*
> *against the wall of a raised churchyard in the foreground, while*
> *he stands holding her hands as he seized them, half in*
> *bewilderment and half guarding her from doing herself a hurt.*
> *These are the chief things in the picture which is to be called*
> *"Found" and for which my sister Maria has found me a most*
> *lovely motto from Jeremiah: "I remember Thee, the kindness of*
> *thy youth, the love of thine espousals. . . ."*[2]

Yet the complete significance of the work and its multiple implications and relationships are anything but straightforward—are highly problematic, in fact—and can best be illuminated by examining it in a variety of perspectives. First of all, situating *Found* in the context of a whole range of nineteenth-century attempts to invent a secular pictorial imagery of the fallen woman, a pressing social and moral, as well as often personal, contemporary issue, helps reveal the unconscious, or what might be termed the ideological assumptions Rossetti makes about his subject, as well as the vividly personal aspects of his inflection of it. Second, *Found* will be examined in relation to another Pre-Raphaelite's interpretation of the fallen-woman theme, Holman Hunt's *Awakening Conscience,* to which Rossetti's painting may be considered in some ways a paradoxically contradictory pendant, and for which I believe another work of Rossetti's supplied at least part of the inspiration. Third, the sources and the formulation of the pictorial structure of *Found* will be examined. Fourth, it will be considered in relation to the meanings

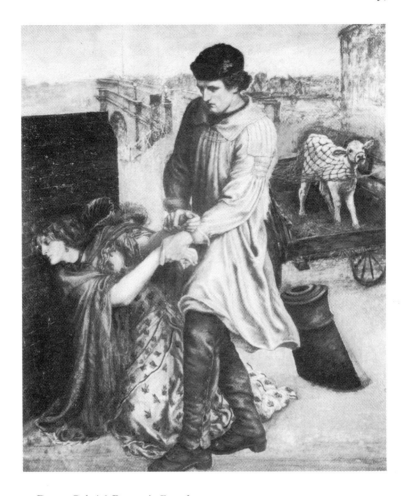

1. Dante Gabriel Rossetti. *Found*

it may have had in the artist's personal history. And finally, I will demonstrate that the fact that Rossetti was a poet as well as a painter, and dealt with the theme of the fallen woman in verse as well as in pictures, has little or no relevance to the major features of structure or expression—as opposed to the mere "story" or the iconographic details—of *Found*. Indeed, the fact that Rossetti was inspired by his own "Jenny," turned to William Bell Scott's poetry for subject matter or for details of symbolism, and in turn looked to his own painting for inspiration in his later sonnet, "Found," seems to me in no way to imply that poems and pictures do more than simply explicate one another, or that they are locked together semantically or syntactically. Millais's *Ophelia* was not "semantically or syntactically locked" to the verses of Shakespeare's *Hamlet*, which inspired it and which it so faithfully reproduces, any more than Keats's "Ode to a Grecian Urn" was structurally or syntactically related to the principles of Greek vase painting. On the contrary, I should say that in *Found*, above all his other paintings, Rossetti's strategies are those of the painters of his time. He directs his attention firmly to suitable pictorial precedents for his composition, and to the task—a relatively conventional one in the nineteenth century and one that preoccupied the majority of artists of the period, from Delacroix or Couture to Hunt or Millais—of creating a suitable visual imagery, a meaningful pictorial structure, for relatively complex ideas or issues or narratives. It is a pictorial mode that has often been called "literary" since the time of Fry and Bell (although in actuality it is no more literary than film, which also attempts to do some of the same things by means of visual images rather than words). In other words, I think that there is nothing particularly "poetic" or even literary about *Found*, or indeed anything about it that particularly marks it off from other similar narrative or morally meaningful nineteenth-century works as the work of a painter who is also a poet.

First, let us consider the general context of "fallen-woman" imagery, which I believe is critical to a reading of the painting. In the background, for any English artist of the nineteenth century turning to the subject of the prostitute—and especially for the Pre-Raphaelites, who were conscious of being both English and moral at the same time—lay the visual precedent of Hogarth; and for Rossetti especially lay the precedent of Blake, like himself a poet and a painter; and more particularly, in the case of *Found*, Blake's "London."[3] Yet already in the late eighteenth and early nineteenth centuries, Hogarth's brisk setting-forth of the inexorable working of natural law to punish folly and sensuality, as well as Blake's apocalyptic vision of innocence inexorably corrupted by greed and the great city, had been considerably softened by sentimentality and humanitarianism. By the nineteenth century it was readily conceded that a woman might fall as much through need as through greed, and that she might redeem herself through repentance and subsequent reintegration into the family. Indeed, the institution of the family plays an increasingly important role, either as a foil to rehabilitation or as the instrument of it, in the imagery of the fallen woman in the nineteenth century. As early as 1789, George Morland, in his *Laetitia* series (engraved by John Raphael Smith), which demonstrated the downfall of an innocent country girl, had substituted a happy ending for Hogarth's grim finale. In *The Fair Penitent* the heroine, still fallen—and a literal fall seems a sine qua non of this imagery—but more in confusion than depravity, is welcomed back into the bosom of the family. The setting of innocence here is pointedly rural, as opposed to the equally pointed urbanism of the setting of sin in the same series. The theme of redemption through a return to the family and native village, of rehabilitation through rural felicity and the acceptance of the country girl's "natural" humble position in society, had considerable currency in French popular imagery of the early nineteenth century, where, merging with the more traditional, serial *images populaires* of the prodigal son, it emerged as the topos of the *fille coupable*—the guilty daughter—in a wide range of variations. In *La Vie d'une femme* of 1836 [2], an anonymous wood engraving from *chez* Pillot in Paris, the kneeling pose generally associated with falling in the feminine is reserved for prayer or penitence. The more sophisticated lithograph series, *La Vie d'une jolie fille* of 1847, pendant to *La Vie d'un joli garçon* by Jules David, is more obvious in its filiation from Hogarth, and obviously intended for a more worldly clientele, both French and English; there are many other examples, all of which stress return to the family as the "solution" to the fall. Lurking behind most of the fallen-woman imagery of the nineteenth century is the sometimes explicit but more often unspoken assumption that the only honorable position for a young woman is her role within the family: the role of daughter, wife, and mother. Speaking figuratively, one might say that behind every crouched figure of a fallen woman there stands the eminently upright one of the angel in the house.

This conventional contrast is used several times to good effect

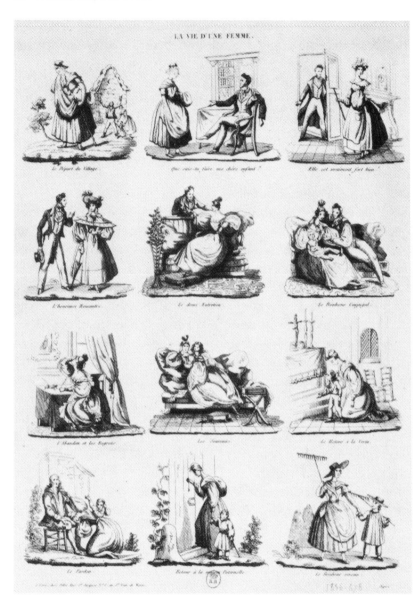

2. *La Vie d'une femme.* Wood engraving

by William Bell Scott in his long poem on the fallen-woman theme, "Rosabell," one of Rossetti's presumptive sources for the subject of *Found*.[4] In section II of "Rosabell," the prostitute's hard fate is contrasted with the domestic felicity of the good, humble woman whom her childhood sweetheart married instead: their cosy domestic interior—the husband doffing his shoes before the fire, the child sleeping, the wife "sewing tiny frills that it shall wear," the "window and curtain and the light"[5]—is pointedly contrasted with the cold, rainy, outdoor setting chosen for the description of fallen Rosabell in the verses that follow: "Down the wet pavement gleam the lamps,/While the cold wind whistles past;/A distant heel rings hurrying home,/It lessens into stillness now,/And she is left alone again. . . ."[6] The implicit loss of domestic happiness, the irrevocable exclusion from the joys of the family, is signified in quite subtle pictorial terms by Rossetti, in the contrast he creates between the group in the left foreground foiled by wall and graveyard and the shuttered house—home as seen from the vantage point of the pariah —as well as the nest-building sparrows to the right.

The connection between the opposing terms of family and fallen woman and the sinister threat that woman's unregulated sexual activity was felt to offer the bulwark of Victorian paternal authoritarianism, the home, are nowhere given more explicit visual expression than in Augustus Egg's three-part painting entitled (probably erroneously) *Past and Present*, exhibited at the Royal Academy in 1858.[7] Here, in part one (see Figure 10 in Chapter 1), the Fall is literally enacted in a middle-class domestic interior—a setting with ironic reminiscences of the *Arnolfini Wedding Portrait;* the impact of the fall, emphasized by the half-eaten apple on the table, is re-echoed in the tumbling of the children's house of cards. The awfulness of the wife's lapse is given added emphasis by the space chosen for the unfolding of the tragedy, the parlor, cella of that domestic temple which it is woman's natural duty to guard. The wife and mother's adultery shatters the order of nature; the sacred place is profaned: this is perhaps the most serious order of transgression in the canon of bourgeois morality. Indeed, there is no place for the erring wife to go but out; she must be sent forth from the parlor-paradise, an eventuality suggested by the open door in the background and reiterated by the print of the Expulsion on the wall behind the fallen figure. The outside, the city exterior, becomes the literal as well as the metaphoric place of the fallen woman in the third painting of Egg's trilogy: here the fallen wife, who has obviously lost her money and her position in the world along with her virtue, clasping the fruit of her sin in her arms, and still crouching, looks wistfully but hopelessly back at her former home from beneath a dry arch, an outside-inside dichotomy that was suggested by the first painting in the series and, in less obvious form, in Rossetti's painting as well, where outsideness, with its threats, its very contradiction of being at home in the world, and the city setting are the natural space of the fallen woman.

Indeed, the fallen woman thrust from home is the explicit theme of at least two paintings of the period: the English Richard Redgrave's melodramatic *Outcast* of 1851 and the more sober, realistic, and restrained Russian work, representing a pregnant girl forced out of her lodgings, *Thrown Out (At the Station)* of 1883, by Nikolai Alexandrovitch Iaroshenko (1846–1899).[8]

At the same time that the fate of the fallen woman was tellingly contrasted with the sacred security of home and family in nineteenth-century imagery of erring womanhood, a realistic account began to be taken of the economic factors involved in women's fall from virtue, with the sympathetic, often sentimental setting forth of the tragic consequences of sheer, desperate need. One of the most striking of such representations is George Frederic Watts's *Found Drowned*, painted about 1848–50—brief years of social radicalism on the part of the artist as well as for Europe as a whole—one of four paintings Watts dedicated at the time to the depiction of the helpless suffering of the poor, and of poor women especially. *Found Drowned* represents a suicide washed up under the arch of Waterloo Bridge. The interpretation of the causes of the young woman's suicide would seem obvious to the nineteenth-century viewer, and were manifestly connected with Thomas Hood's widely known poem on the subject, "The Bridge of Sighs" of 1844, which is closely related: the victim was understood to have done away with herself because of poverty and consequent falling, for some women still a fate worse than death. Watts, like Hood, meant to arouse feelings of sympathy

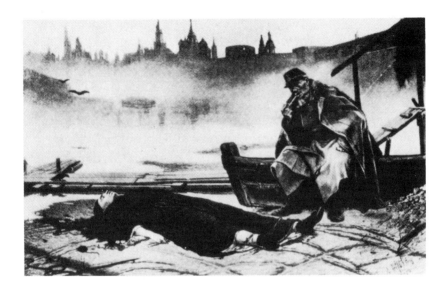

3. Vassily Grigorievitch Perov. *The Drowned Woman*

and compassion rather than condemnation; his painting may be considered a visual equivalent of Hood's admonition to "Take her up instantly,/Loving not loathing./Touch her not scornfully;/Think of her mournfully,/Gently and humanly;/Not of the stains of her,/All that remains of her/Now is pure womanly...."[9] Vassily Grigorievitch Perov's *Drowned Woman* [3] of 1867 seems strikingly related to Watts's work (or Hood's poem), but it is far more explicit in its ironic contrast between the pathos of the young girl's suicide and the indifference of society, implied by the presence of the constable who smokes his pipe phlegmatically to the right of the young victim; and Perov is far more concerned to specify the working-class origins of the drowned girl in details of dress and setting. Obviously in this case, an unjust and indifferent social order, rather than the fallen woman, is meant to be the object of censure.

Certainly the economic determinants of prostitution were openly discussed and strongly deplored in England in the decade of the fifties. A long, well-documented, and by no means pussyfooting article on the subject by W. R. Greg appeared in 1850. Citing the bible of prostitution research, A. J. B. Parent-Duchâtelet's *De la Prostitution dans la ville de Paris* (first published in 1836 and issued in new editions for years) as well as the results of the current investigations into the lives of the London poor by Henry Mayhew, then appearing in the form of letters to the *Morning Chronicle,* Greg states unequivocally that "poverty is the chief determining cause which drives women into prostitution in England as in France."[10] A small sepia drawing from Rossetti's own circle, John Millais's *Virtue and Vice,* signed and dated 1853—the year of the earliest dated compositional study for *Found*—could illustrate Mayhew's or Greg's vivid testimony about the situation of women "slop-workers" (pieceworkers), whose wages were so pitifully low that they were forced to sell themselves to keep themselves, or at times their children, from starving. Millais, despite the symbolic dramatization of the momentous choice, which transforms the temptress at the left into a kind of female Satan, has realistically rendered the bleakness of the garret and the thinness and exhaustion of the young slop-worker, and has underlined the economic determination of falling by the parcel of shirts on the floor to the right and the notice near the window headed "distressed needlewoman." It is perhaps relevant to point out that in the earliest version of *Found,* the young woman fallen to the pavement is thin and shabby-looking rather than tawdry and voluptuous; like Millais's seamstress, she is dressed poorly and modestly, suggesting that she too had been driven to her fate rather than freely choosing it. Millais has also provided an obvious compositional parallel with Rossetti's original conception of *Found* in his own pen and ink drawing of the same year, *Accepted,* as well as a kind of moral counterweight to Rossetti's drawing. *Accepted,* like *Found,* had a basis in a disturbing personal relationship with the opposite sex: it is one of a series of drawings dealing with the troubled interaction between a man and a woman dating from the period of Millais's courtship of Effie Ruskin.

Yet perhaps no work is more closely intertwined with Rossetti's *Found* and his very conception of the fallen woman than Holman Hunt's *Awakening Conscience* [4], signed and dated 1853, exhibited at the Royal Academy in 1854. Despite their striking differences of

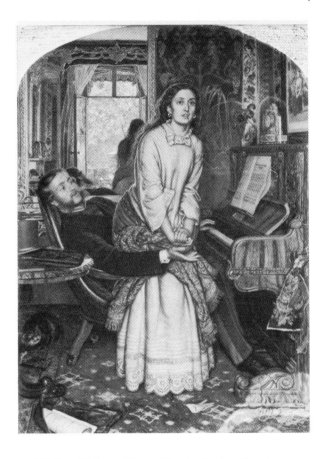

4. William Holman Hunt. *The Awakening Conscience*

interpretation and structure, or perhaps because of them, one can see these works as pendants, opposing visions of a single moral issue: rising versus falling, salvation versus damnation, Christian optimism versus Christian or crypto-Christian despair, the larger oppositions in both cases growing out of intimate personal experience, probably involving Annie Miller, and couched in the pictorial language of realism. Like Rossetti, Hunt reinforces the credibility of his pains-taking visual realism with an equally painstaking scaffolding of sym-bolic incident: at the crucial instant of conscience awakening, a cat releases a bird beneath the table, and light—reflected in the mirror in the background—quite literally dawns in the unspoiled garden outside the St. John's Wood sitting room. That parlor's unsavoriness is attested by such elements as the print *Christ and the Woman Taken in Adultery* on the wall, the dozing cupids on the clock, the birds stealing grapes in the wall design, as well as by what Ruskin admiringly described as the "fatal newness" of the furniture. The volume of Noel Humphrey's *Origin and Progress of the Art of Writing* on the table may be a covert reference to Hunt's educational program for his "fiancée," Annie Miller, the original model for the painting. Certainly it is no accident that the young woman experiencing moral epiphany has rings on every finger *but* the third finger of her left hand.

Like Rossetti's, Hunt's work was no doubt originally based on a creative misunderstanding of Hogarth: perhaps of *The Lady's Last Stake,* as John Duncan MacMillan recently suggested;[11] probably by Hogarth's paired engravings, *Before* and *After,* with their emphatic lap-sitting, rising, and falling in an *intérieur moralisé;*[12] and doubtless by *The Harlot's Progress* with the hopeful ending of nineteenth-century sentimentality substituted for the original one. Like Rossetti—as we shall see—Hunt turned to the precedent of Jan van Eyck, specifically to the *Arnolfini Portrait* in the National Gallery for his inspiration in the setting and perhaps for a certain validation of Pre-Raphaelite authenticity, for a reassuringly primitive freshness of feeling, as well as a sincerity of execution, although he, like Rossetti, drew on more conventionally sophisticated sources as well. It would seem likely that Hunt made use of an engraving after Charles Le Brun's *Repentant Magdalene Renouncing All the Vanities of the World* for the relatively rare motif of upward mobility on the part of the fallen woman.[13]

Rossetti, too, could not fail to associate contemporary fall with the precedent of the Bible: both his elaborate drawing and his sonnet, "Mary Magdalene at the Door of Simon the Pharisee," of 1858, are obviously related to the theme of *Found.* Like Rossetti, Hunt had been moved to pictorial action by literary incident. When considering his subject, Hunt said, he had been touched by the description of Peggotty's search for the outcast Emily in *David Copperfield,* first published in 1849–1850.[14] Yet more likely, as for Rossetti, the direct inspiration for *The Awakening Conscience* was visual rather than literary, in this instance Phiz's illustration of 1849, not of the search for Emily but of the finding of the prostitute Martha in the same novel. Topoi from both Rossetti's and Hunt's paintings of fallen women seem to find echoes in the work of a later artist obsessed with problematic sexuality, Edvard Munch: *The Cry* of 1893, now in the Oslo Municipal Collection, seems an intensification of the implications of the lonely figure on the bridge behind the main incident in *Found;* and the adolescent girl in *Puberty* of 1894, now in the National Gallery, Oslo, repeats, with changed and ominous emphasis, the protective, traditional gesture of *pudeur* suggested by the protagonist of the *Awakening Conscience,* a gesture perhaps transmitted through an etching by Félicien Rops of 1886.[15]

The fallen-woman imagery of Hunt and Rossetti may have an even more specific connection: indeed, Hunt's painting may be directly dependent upon a Rossettian prototype for its most characteristic features. In the letter to Hunt of 30 January 1855 describing *Found,* Rossetti prefaces his description with the following remark: "The subject had been sometime designed before you left England [that is, before 16 January 1854, when Hunt started off for the Holy Land via Paris and Alexandria] and will be thought, by anyone who sees it when (and if) finished, to follow in the wake of your 'Awakened Conscience', but not by yourself, as you know I had long had in view subjects taking the same direction as my present one."[16] Despite the frequency of Pre-Raphaelite squabbles over precedence, and the incontrovertible fact that the *terminus ante quem* for the *Awakening Conscience* is 1853, the year of the earliest dated complete project for *Found,* it is significant that Hunt, who had originally, in the 1905 edition of his *Pre-Raphaelitism,* dated *his* first thoughts for the *Awakening Conscience* to 1851, revised this date to 1853 in the edition of 1913.[17] But there is more substantial evidence that Rossetti provided the pictorial inspiration for the basic conception as well as many of the characteristic details of the *Awakening Conscience:* this evidence is Rossetti's small pen and ink drawing, similar in its moral, if not modern, subject: *Hesterna Rosa* [5]. This little drawing (which Rossetti reworked as a watercolor in 1865),[18] although signed and dated in the lower left corner "1853," is nevertheless confusingly

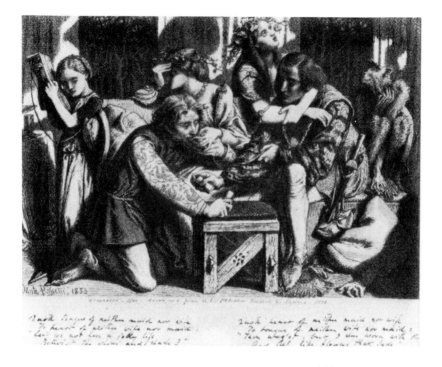

5. Dante Gabriel Rossetti. *Hesterna Rosa*

inscribed at its foot, "composed—1850—drawn, and given to his
P.R. Brother Frederic G. Stephens—1853," which suggests an earlier
origin. It is certainly not a contemporary subject. (The drawing was
intended as an illustration of Elena's song from Sir Henry Taylor's
play *Philip van Artevelde,* the verses of which are inscribed at the
bottom of the Tate drawing.) Nevertheless, *Hesterna Rosa* proposes
the major themes of Hunt's fallen-woman painting. Like the *Awakening Conscience,* it demonstrates the power of music, an art traditionally associated with erotic temptation,[19] to awaken conscience
by recalling childlike innocence, personified by the little girl playing
and listening to the lute at the left. She is the embodiment of the
memories of childhood innocence and subsequent "holy resolve"
aroused by the playing of "Oft in the Stilly Night" in Hunt's
painting. In *Hesterna Rosa,* too, the conscience-stricken woman is,

like Hunt's, entangled with an uncaring, shallow male companion, who, continuing his play, provides a foil for her sudden change of heart. The contrast of inside and outside, the crowded, body-packed realm of sin opposed to the pure realm of nature outside the windows, is present in both works, although much further developed in Hunt's, as is the symbolic significance of animals—the ape in Rossetti's picture, the cat in Hunt's. Even the telltale symptom of a moral as well as physical carelessness in the dropped gloves appears in both works. *Hesterna Rosa*, then, may have been what Rossetti had in mind when he alerted Hunt in the beginning of 1855 to "subjects long in view" that took the same direction as *Found*.

And what of *Found* itself, or, more specifically, the drawings for it of 1853 and ca. 1855? These provide us with information about Rossetti's intentions, of which the incompleteness of the painting deprives us. Of course, the carefully described brickwork in the oil version, the later substitution of Fanny Cornforth for the original model (possibly Annie Miller),[20] and the deliberate change in the skirt and smock from chaste, "primitive" restraint to emotionally charged Baroque surge, flow, and flutter have a significance of their own in the interpretation of the imaginative evolution of the theme. Yet in neither the earlier nor the later versions do I think that the structure of *Found* is significantly bound to Rossetti's strategies as a poet when dealing with the theme of the fallen woman.

True, *Found* is related to poetic precedent in some of its details, first of all, to that of William Bell Scott's "Rosabell," which, during the course of a visit Rossetti made to Newcastle during the summer of 1853, Scott evidently retitled "Mary Ann," a name Rossetti felt was more indicative of the humble rank of the heroine. "Rosabell," which Rossetti claimed to have altered substantially in conjunction with its author,[21] may indeed have suggested the general idea of rural innocence corrupted by the temptations of the city, the abandoned farmer-boy sweetheart, and the cold, isolated outdoor setting of *Found;* but Scott's poem did not include a meeting of the erring woman with her former sweetheart, although Rossetti evidently suggested that Scott alter his poem to include this incident. Portions of Scott's long narrative poem could even more easily be related to themes in Millais's or Hunt's paintings of fallen women than to

Found. Rather than *Found*, Rossetti's watercolor of 1857, *The Gate of Memory*, depicting a prostitute standing under an archway watching a group of dancing children who remind her of her own lost innocence, must be considered the work most closely related to Scott's poem; indeed, the watercolor is an illustration of a specific scene described in the poem.[22] Nor do I think that there is any substantive structural relation between *Found* and Rossetti's poem on the fallen-woman theme, "Jenny," which was first begun in 1847–48 (when it was engagingly awkward, openly indebted to Blake, and unabashedly sexy), published in greatly modified form in the edition of 1870 of the *Poems*, and reworked as late as the edition of 1881.[23] Certain descriptive features of the poem do appear in the pictorial work—the "long drooping throat" attributed to Jenny (but then again, to what Rossetti female would it *not* be attributed?) and visible in the heroine of the painting; the symbolic rose-patterning of the fallen woman's dress (in the painting, to be sure, not the earlier drawings); the early wagon, and the London sparrows (which would, in the drawing, appear to be engaged in nest-building rather than merely "clamouring," as in the poem). Despite these parallels, however, "Jenny" is remarkably different, both literally and figuratively, from its supposed visual equivalent, *Found*.[24] What is lacking in the painting is the complexity of attitude, as well as the multiplicity of viewpoints, of the poem: the latter was severely criticized by Ruskin when Rossetti showed him "Jenny" in 1859;[25] the poem's complexity was created by the mediation of the theme of the fallen woman through the consciousness of the young male narrator. If the poem "Jenny" may be said to be "about" any one thing, it is less about the fate of a young prostitute—who, in the poem, never encounters her childhood sweetheart—than about the inner life of the sophisticated young narrator, certainly identifiable with the poet himself, and his meditations upon sex, sin, men and women, the paradoxical contrast between the "good" woman and the "bad one," the nature of time and the nature of atonement. Indeed, so subjective, even egocentric, is the poem that at the critical point the actual Jenny fades from view, becoming in rapid succession a "cipher of man's changeless sum of lust," a riddle, and, finally and most daringly, a stimulus for a simile in which lust is likened to "a toad within a stone."[26] The striking freedom of association, compounded equally of psychological flow and sharp disjunctions of tone and mood, the shifts of distance and vantage point, the ambivalence of the attitude, compounded of compassion and condescension (strategies at least partly inspired by Browning, whom Rossetti still greatly admired at the time)[27]—all these are completely foreign to the painting. So is the crucial sense of being *within* the flexible space of an individual subjectivity—a possibility, after all, not completely unavailable to painting—instead of being situated at a fixed distance from an external event, which is the spatial assumption of *Found*. And certainly, if we compare *Found* with the later sonnet in which, we may speculate, Rossetti attempted to articulate more fully the implications of the painting he was never able to finish, we find that, on the contrary, Rossetti has chosen to simplify and exclude much that is suggested by the painting. Further, by emphasizing the contrast between light and dark as a moral metaphor of despair he makes the sonnet sound far more forceful and unequivocal in its pessimism than the picture for which it exists as a kind of late-life gloss. In cutting off the fallen woman from possible redemption, the final line, "Leave me—I do not know you—go away,"[28] is absolute in a way that the painting is not, with its brightening dawn suggesting "peace with forgiveness. . .," to borrow the words of F. G. Stephens.[29]

In short, I do not believe that Rossetti's poems on the fallen woman and the visual imagery of *Found* exhibit any of those essential structural analogies that, for example, Roman Jakobson has demonstrated to exist in related verse and pictures in the case of three other poet painters, Blake, the Douanier Rousseau, and Paul Klee.[30] In *Found*, on the contrary, Rossetti, like most other painters of the nineteenth century and before, attempted to body forth moral meaning and personal feeling, to create a structure of space rich in significance and implicit temporality, by means of the most effective visual signifiers possible—in pictorial not in poetic language, in short. To achieve this end he turned to suitable pictorial precedents and to the direct study of nature, a practice strongly recommended by Ruskin, whose opinion certainly counted for something with Rossetti at the time, and one followed assiduously by his fellow

Pre-Raphaelites, especially during the early fifties. Although such scrupulous realism is not usual in Rossetti's oeuvre, in the case of *Found* he took the view of Blackfriars' Bridge from his own window at Chatham Place; struggled with the brick wall—brick by brick— at Chiswick; and painted the calf and cart, "like Albert Dürer, hair by hair," as Ford Madox Brown impatiently remarked, while staying with the Browns at Finchley in 1854, a prolonged bout of painting that strained the friendship almost to the breaking point.[31]

If *Found* is full of messages, stuffed with narrative implications, it is no more so than innumerable other paintings of its time and place. Even the inscription of a pointed biblical text on the completed drawing, which might suggest an essential connection between words and picture—"I remember thee;/The kindness of thy youth, the love of thy betrothal"—is by no means unique to the poet Rossetti; Hunt, for example, whose major literary achievement is the voluminous and certainly far from poetic *Pre-Raphaelitism and the Pre-Raphaelite Brotherhood*, inscribed the *Awakening Conscience* with a similarly apposite biblical tag on the frame.[32] Indeed, with respect to the structure of *Found*, one might say that Rossetti is less constrained by poetry, or by his conception of the poetic or the "musical"—that is, the decorative—than he is in most of his other pictorial works.

As is true of so many other nineteenth-century paintings, perspective, or more specifically, the pictorial suggestion of deep space, is deployed to suggest moral and temporal factors impossible to convey more literally on the static, two-dimensional surface of the canvas. In a manner analogous, although in no way similar, to that in which Couture suggests a morally purer past by means of a perspective vista in his *Romans of the Decadence* of 1847 or Goya the *via crucis*–like progression from the everyday to the horrific by the deeply shadowed perspective in his *Execution of the Madrileños*, so Rossetti has deployed the turning vista of Blackfriars' Bridge to suggest the past and the future, the moral meaning and the painful consequences of falling in the feminine. Spatial divisions are the meaningful indexes of moral and spiritual temperature throughout: the churchyard wall, separating upright from fallen; the bollard, separating purity—the symbolic, sacrificial white calf—from corruption; the geometric blocks of the pavement separating the spiritually problematic group in the foreground from the simple, old irregularities of the cobblestones in the middle distance, a separation emphasized by the prominence of the bollard—a threatening boundary, suggestive of both phallus and gravestone in its conformation; the sharp orthogonal border dividing pavement from gutter, to which falling is materially related; the bars of the graveyard, separating death from life, yet suggesting the imminence of mortality, just as the mesh of the white calf's net suggests that life is enmeshed by death, that innocence is doomed to destruction. Perhaps most important of all is the bridge dividing city from country, virginal past from fallen present—the bridge whose significance is further heightened, not in the unfinished painting, but in the complete drawings, by the moving presence of an isolated, anonymous female figure. The figure on the bridge is an emblem too of the future alienation of the fallen woman that carries an implication of contemplated suicide: the little figure seems to be walking close to the stairway leading down to the river, and would produce ominous reverberations in viewers familiar with the precedents of Hood and Watts. Coincidentally, the Russian painter Vassily Grigorievitch Perov, creator of *The Drowned Girl* of 1867, actually executed a study, *Young Woman Throwing Herself into the Moscow River,* of about the same date, a work that seems a fulfillment of the suggestion offered by Rossetti's painting; and Rossetti himself dealt with the theme of the betrayed woman who commits suicide by throwing herself and her baby into the river in a poem of 1871, "The River's Record."[33]

In quite idiosyncratic ways, Rossetti has called on past pictorial precedent in envisioning his modern subject, precedents that he radically alters to his purposes, or in the case of the central illumination offered by Hogarth's *Harlot's Progress* [6], that were inevitably altered by the pressures of nineteenth-century compassion, sentimentality, and doubts about the inevitable workings of natural law —in short, by the basic assumptions of nineteenth-century ideology itself. In *Found,* Rossetti has compressed the narrative sequence of Hogarth's serial morality—the "progress"—into a single pregnant image, substituting evocative spatial expansion for brisk narrative sequentiality, or, in other words, suggestive depth for explicit suc-

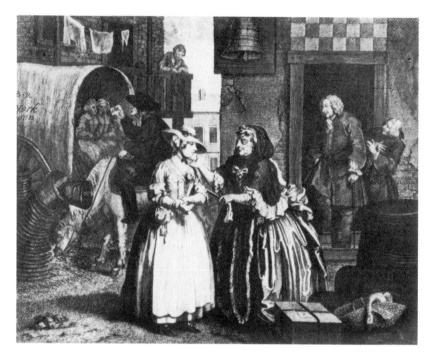

6. William Hogarth. *The Harlot's Progress.* Engraving

cession in time. And he has substituted a reduced range of symbolic
reference for Hogarth's burgeoning richness of descriptive detail.
The rural origins of the harlot, for example, specified in Hogarth by
her arrival on the stagecoach in the first plate of the series, is simply
suggested in Rossetti by the calf and the bridge, as well as by the
country dress of her would-be rescuer. The inevitable downfall and
death of the harlot, spelled out with considerable circumstantial
detail and social concreteness, stage by stage in Hogarth's work, is
simply implied in Rossetti's, by the pose, the expression of shame,
or even anguish in the head in the oil version (modelled by Fanny
Cornforth in a bit of "ironic typecasting"),[34] the woman on the
bridge, and, most explicitly, by the graveyard, which in the earlier
drawing reveals a tombstone in the corner with the inscription,
just legible, "There is joy . . . the Angels in he . . . one sinner

that . . .," a message of faint hope that, contradicting Hogarth's moral, perhaps softens the sense of spiritual as well as physical death suggested by the graveyard itself. Even the precedent for symbolic animals is found in Hogarth, although with the typical difference that it is the silly goose, the lecherous monkey, and the sensual cat that are depicted, rather than the innocent and pathetic netted calf.

For the specific setting of two large foreground figures against a city vista with a bridge in the background, Rossetti probably turned to the entirely appropriate Pre-Raphaelite precedent of Jan van Eyck, whose *Madonna and the Chancellor Rolin* he had admired when he had visited Paris with Hunt in 1849,[35] and which probably served again as an inspiration for his illustration of Saint Cecilia and the Angel for "The Palace of Art" in the Moxon *Tennyson* of 1857.[36]

For the two foreground figures of *Found* he turned, perhaps

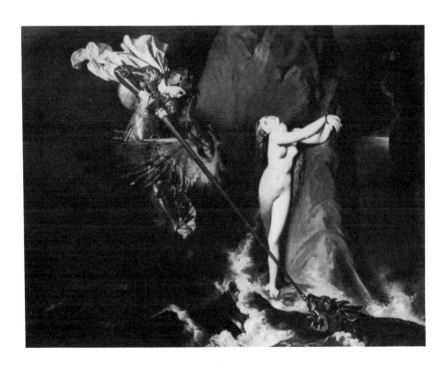

7. Jean-Auguste-Dominique Ingres. *Roger Rescuing Angelica*

unconsciously, to a very different pictorial source from the same European trip of 1849: Ingres's *Roger Rescuing Angelica* [7] of 1819, then in the Musée du Luxembourg. The painting had impressed him sufficiently that he sent home two sonnets about it—"Last Visit to the Luxembourg"—in a letter to his brother;[37] the sonnets on Ingres's *Roger Rescuing Angelica* were later published in the *Germ* and reprinted in the *Poems* of 1870.[38] Ingres's painting seems almost calculated to satisfy the contradictory urges of chivalrous purity and sexual lust burning in the breast of the young artist: it provides rich food for erotic fantasy. The poems Rossetti dedicated to it seem, to modern understanding anyway, unequivocal in their sensual relish of Ingres's titillating vision. The impulse behind the imagery is clear: desire is the tenor of every metaphoric expression in the sonnets, from "the spear's lithe stem" to the beast whose "evil length of body chafes at halt," contrasted with the passive but succulent offering of fettered nakedness, "flesh which has the colour of fine pearl," "with loose hair/And throat let back and heartsick trail of limb,"[39] a description that is not far from the pose of the heroine of *Found* herself. One might say that, from one point of view, *Found* is a metamorphosed *Roger Rescuing Angelica* in modern dress, although the outcome is certainly more equivocal. Yet in the earlier versions, where the fallen woman is less flashy, sensual, and fancily attired, the abortive outcome of the drover's chivalrous and compassionate gesture is not as clearly articulated as it becomes in the final version, where the conflict between the two is heightened and active; and of course the impossibility of the harlot's being saved is made clear in the later sonnet "Found." Different though *Found* may be in many ways from *Roger Rescuing Angelica*, in both, desirable young women are prisoners of sex—one is a real prisoner of a metaphorical monster sex; the other a metaphorical prisoner of real sexual enslavement. Ultimately, it is the fallen woman's heart rather than merely her body that is "locked" in Rossetti's final reinterpretation of the theme in the sonnet "Found," and for this sort of imprisonment there would seem to be no possible rescue in the form of man's good will or chivalric impulse. In a sense, *Found* is finally seen as a sort of dark Annunciation, a perverse revision of *Ecce Ancilla Domini!* [8]—there also a cowering female is set in opposition to a

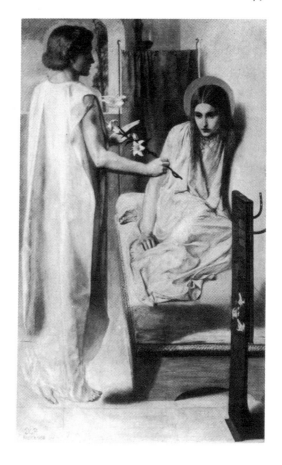

8. Dante Gabriel Rossetti.
Ecce Ancilla Domini! (The Annunciation)

towering male figure—but here, the fallen woman refuses to
"know" the messenger and sends him away instead of receiving glad
tidings.

Found, then, is a palimpsest of motifs and motivations: it exists
as an image that evolved over time, and it is possible that Rossetti's
own interpretations of it were multiple. Certainly, on one level,
Rossetti meant to imply that salvation for the fallen woman could
take place only in distant biblical times, through the intervention of

Christ, and that no possibility of redemption is possible for the modern prostitute. This interpretation is certainly suggested by a comparison of *Found* and its accompanying sonnet with the sonnet and drawing of *Mary Magdalene at the Door of Simon the Pharisee* of 1848.[40] Such an attitude was morally convenient for Rossetti, as it was for most men of his time, in that it exempts actual human beings, mere sensual men, from any responsibility in the situation: falling in the feminine is considered a metaphysical absolute rather than a social and ethical issue that might be dealt with and changed by means of human effort and action. The term "fallen" is not reversible; the attitude producing it ends as helpless pity or contempt; at best, as the protectiveness of a superior being for an inferior one. Yet, on another level, it would be a mistake to read the fallen woman in this painting simply as an emblem of Rossetti's attitude toward women: on a deeper level, perhaps, it also reflects his attitude toward himself. Seen at the end of his life, *Found* may be understood as a paradigm of Rossetti's own conflict-ridden existence, beginning with an idea of himself as the "preux chevalier" dedicated to rescue and the highest sort of artistic achievement, the most ideal way of life, and ending with despair and disillusion. In this light, the fallen "fair woman" might be considered not merely Jenny or Rosabell or Annie Miller or Fanny Cornforth, but an aspect of the artist himself—his *anima,* a subject he depicted in a drawing of 1880 flying triumphantly with her fourteen-stringed harp,[41] here fallen and drooping.

If a woman has indeed figured as "Rossetti's icon for the artistic soul in the act of creation,"[42] then the figure of a woman could also be an image of his despair, his sense of the self—more specifically, the creative self—shut off from the possibility of help or redemption. Indeed, his attitude toward his own work was strangely ambiguous, especially toward his painting, which he tended to look down on in comparison with his poetry. "I wish one could live by writing poetry. I think I'd see painting d—d if one could," he wrote to Ford Madox Brown in 1871.[43] Later in life, Rossetti had increasing recourse to "replicas" to raise money quickly; increasingly, he lost respect for his art, referring to *The Blessed Damozel,* once the very symbol of his moral and erotic idealism, as the "Blasted Damdozel," the "Blowed Damozel," or even more crudely, as the "Bdy Dam."[44] In a letter to Frederic James Shields of 1869, he declares that he has now begun to rate his poetry above his painting, describing it as the art "in which I have done no pot-boiling at any rate. So," he continues, "I am grateful to that art and nourish against the other that base grudge which we bear against those whom we have treated shabbily."[45] Rossetti had treated *Found* shabbily indeed, complaining about it, boasting of the new patrons he had seduced into making down-payments for it, never completing it: indeed, his attitude toward the painting began to resemble the attitude that he might have had toward an ill-treated woman. The painting of the fallen woman can almost be seen as a synecdoche of Rossetti's disillusion with painting and with himself as a painter. Rossetti made explicit the analogy between an artist and a prostitute in a letter to Ford Madox Brown of 1873: "I have often said that to be an artist is just the same thing as to be a whore, as far as dependence on the whims and fancies of individuals is concerned."[46]

Not only, then, might Rossetti in later years feel deep sexual conflict and guilt, feel himself to be in some way "fallen": he was an exemplary "homme de mauvaise foi" in Sartrean terms, as a nineteenth-century man of strong sensuality who at the same time believed fervently in some kind of ideal of goodness but could rarely bring himself to act upon this belief. But he also might feel identified with the image of the fallen woman in *Found* in still another way. To return to the verbal analysis with which this discussion opened, "to prostitute oneself," like "to fall" is also an irreversible verbal form: for a man to prostitute himself means not to sell sex for money, as it does in the case of a woman, but rather—the fate worse than death in the masculine, for the artist above all—to debase one's art for money, to sell one's talent, to "sell out," in short. Surely this sense of moral failure, of "selling out," or perhaps of "overselling" hangs over the troubled history of *Found* and at least in part accounts for its unfinished state. Although Rossetti claimed in a letter of 1881 that the "eternal *Found* picture is really getting done:—the figures close upon finish . . . ," it passed unfinished into the possession of William Graham after the artist's death, whereupon Burne-Jones and possibly Dunn did further work on it.[47] Sick, suffering, and miserable, in 1881 Rossetti seems to have sensed the nothingness lying in wait beyond the palace of art, behind the dreams of love and creation, and he turned backward to memory, still undecided: "Is Memory most of miseries miserable, or the one flower of ease in bitterest hell?" he asked.[48] His answer, the painting *Mnemosyne* (Bancroft Collection, Delaware Art Museum), fails to answer the question, but simply replies with another kind of mystery. In a sense, *Found* should be considered less a key to Rossetti's ultimate feelings about sex, women, salvation, or the self than as evidence of the deep-seated conflicts and contradictions he experienced about all of them: it should perhaps be judged less as a work of art than as a document of unfulfilled aspirations.

Bibliography of Frequently Cited Works

Bandelin, Susan B., " 'Allegorizing on One's Own Hook': Works before 1863," *Dante Gabriel Rossetti and the Double Work of Art*, exhibition catalogue, Yale University Art Gallery, New Haven, 1976, 44–45.

Doughty, Oswald, *Dante Gabriel Rossetti: A Victorian Romantic*, New Haven, 1949.

Rossetti, Dante Gabriel, *Letters of D. G. R.*, ed. O. Doughty and J. R. Wahl, Oxford, 1965.

———, *Poems*, ed. O. Doughty, London, 1957.

Scott, William Bell, "Rosabell: Recitative with Songs," *Autobiographical Notes of William Bell Scott*, ed. W. Minto, New York, 1892, I, 135–52.

Surtees, Virginia, *The Paintings and Drawings of Dante Gabriel Rossetti (1828–1882): A Catalogue Raisonné*, Oxford, 1971.

Notes

1. For a good summary of the history of *Found*, see Virginia Surtees, *The Paintings and Drawings of Dante Gabriel Rossetti (1828–1882): A Catalogue Raisonné*, Oxford, 1971, I, No. 64. Related preparatory studies are discussed by the same author, Nos. 64A to 64R. For illustrations of most of these works, see Surtees, II, pls. 65 through 76. For further information about the history of the paintings and related works, see *Dante Gabriel Rossetti, 1828–1882*, exhibition catalogue, Laing Art Gallery, Newcastle-upon-Tyne, 1971, intro. A. Grieve, No. 17, as well as *Dante Gabriel Rossetti: Painter and Poet*, exhibition catalogue, Royal Academy of Art, London, 1973, No. 70 and Nos. 71 through 84. This article was originally presented at a Rossetti symposium at Yale University in 1976. I am grateful to the participants in the symposium for their suggestions and especially to Professor George Hersey.

2. Cited in Surtees, I, 28.

3. The specific relation to "London" was suggested by A. Grieve, 1971, 5.

4. William Bell Scott, "Rosabell: Recitative with Songs," in W. Minto, ed., *Autobiographical Notes of William Bell Scott*, New York, 1892, I, 135–152.

5. Ibid., 147.

6. Ibid., 148.

7. Anne J. d'Harnoncourt remarks, "The title 'Past and Present' may be the result of misreading Ruskin's Academy notes for 1858, in which a discussion of No. 428, *Past and Present* by Miss A. Blunden, follows immediately after the remarks on Egg's triptych which is given no title"; *"The Awakening Conscience:* A Study of Moral Subject Matter in Pre-Raphaelite Paintings, with a Catalogue of Pictures in the Tate Gallery," M.A. thesis, London, Courtauld Institute of Art, University of London, 1967, Cat. Nos. 3278, 3279, 3280.

8. I am grateful to Alison Hilton for this information.

9. Thomas Hood, "The Bridge of Sighs," *The Complete Poetical Works of Thomas Hood*, New York, 1869, I, 27. For Watts's painting see *G. F. Watts, a Nineteenth Century Phenomenon*, exhibition catalogue, Whitechapel Art Gallery, London, 1974, No. 12. There is a smaller replica of the original that is in the Watts Gallery, in the Walter Art Gallery, Liverpool.

10. [William Rathbone Greg], "Prostitution," *Westminster Review*, LIII, 1850, 461, reprinted in *Prostitution in the Victorian Age: Debates on the Issue from 19th Century Critical Journals*, ed. K. Nield, Westmead, Farnborough (England), 1973, 461.

11. "Holman Hunt's *Hireling Shepherd:* Some Reflections on a Victorian Pastoral," *The Art Bulletin*, LIV, 1972, 195 and fig. 7.

12. For Hogarth's paintings, *Before* (indoor scene) and *After* (indoor scene), ca. 1731?, now in the J. Paul Getty Collection, Art Properties, Inc., see Ronald Paulson, *Hogarth: His Life, Art and Times*, New Haven and London, 1971, I, pls. 89 and 90. For the more richly detailed engraved versions of 1736, see Paulson, *Hogarth's Graphic Works*, New Haven and London, 1965, I, 171–72, Nos. 141 and 142, and II, pls. 152 and 153.

13. This was perhaps Le Brun's best-known painting, thanks to an engraving after it by Edelinck. See *Charles Le Brun, 1619–1690*, Château de Versailles, 1963, 67, No. 25.

14. *William Holman Hunt*, Walker Art Gallery, Liverpool, 1969, intro. M. Bennett, 35, No. 27.

15. Erika Klüsener has suggested the relationship between Munch's *Puberty* and Hunt's *Awakening Conscience*, as well as the intermediary of Felicien Rops's etching, *Le Plus Bel Amour de Don Juan* of 1886: "Das erwachende Bewusstsein: zur Ikonographie der Malerei des 19. Jahrhunderts," *Das Münster*, XXVIII, 1975, 149–52.

16. Cited in Surtees, I, 28.

17. *Hunt*, Liverpool, 1969, 35, No. 27.

18. There is another version of the drawing of 1853 in pen and sepia in the collection of Mrs. Robin Carver, as well as the watercolor, dated 1865, an enlarged replica, in the Bancroft Collection, Wilmington Society of Fine Arts, Delaware. See Surtees, I, Nos. 57, 57A and R. 1.

19. For a discussion of the relation of music-making to eroticism in the imagery of seventeenth-century Dutch painting especially, see A. P. de Mirimonde, "La Musique dans les allégories de l'amour," *Gazette des beaux-arts* XVIII (1966):265–90; LXIX (1967):319–46.

20. For the most detailed information about Annie Miller, mainly in the context of her relation to W. Holman Hunt, see Diana Holman-Hunt, *My Grandfather, His Wives and Loves,* London, 1969. The precise date of the substitution of Fanny Cornforth for the original model of the woman in *Found* is uncertain. Paul Franklin Baum, for instance, in his introduction to *Dante Gabriel Rossetti's Letters to Fanny Cornforth* (Baltimore, 1940, 3–7), tends to support Fanny's own contention that she and Rossetti met in 1856, that she went to his studio the day after their meeting, and, in what are purported to be her own words, "he put my head against the wall and drew it for the head in the calf picture" (p. 4), although Baum admits certain inconsistencies in this account. Surtees, however, would seem to argue for the substitution of the Cornforth head in ca. 1859–61 (see Nos. 64M and 64N), although the date in the catalogue *Dante Gabriel Rossetti: Painter and Poet,* Royal Academy of Arts, London, 1973, for the Birmingham study for the head of the woman modeled by Cornforth (No. 82) is given as ca. 1855–61. Oswald Doughty (*Dante Gabriel Rossetti: A Victorian Romantic,* New Haven, 1949, 251) maintains that "of the two dates, 1856 and 1859, that Fanny herself gave in her two mutually contradictory accounts of her first meeting with Rossetti one is demonstrably a little late," but he does not postulate an exact date for the studies based on Cornforth or the substitution of her head in the oil version of *Found.*

21. In a letter to his mother of 1 July 1853; Oswald Doughty and John Robert Wahl, eds., *Letters of Dante Gabriel Rossetti,* Oxford, 1965, I, 147, No. 116. Scott later changed the title back to its original one (*Autobiographical Notes,* I, 135ff.).

22. See William Bell Scott, "Rosabell," Pt. 13, ll. 16–42, in *Autobiographical Notes,* I, 149–50.

23. The manuscript of the early draft of "Jenny," of 1847–48 is in the collection of the Delaware Art Museum. Rossetti evidently revised and enlarged the poem upon meeting Fanny Cornforth (David Sonstroem, *Rossetti and the Fair Lady,* Middletown, Conn., 1970, 64). William Clyde De Vane ("The Harlot and the Thoughtful Young Man," *Studies in Philology,* XXIX, 1932, 468) asserts that Rossetti kept the poem beside him for twenty-three years, writing and rewriting.

24. For a perceptive analysis of the use of similar iconographic details in "Jenny" and *Found,* see Susan Ball Bandelin, " 'Allegorizing on One's Own Hook': Works Before 1863," *Dante Gabriel Rossetti and the Double Work of Art,* exhibition catalogue, Yale University Art Gallery, New Haven, 1976, 44–45.

25. *Ruskin: Rossetti: Preraphaelitism: Papers 1854 to 1862,* ed. William M. Rossetti, London, 1899, 234. The letter in which Ruskin criticizes "Jenny" is dated ca. 1859 by Sonstroem, n. 1, p. 231.

26. "Jenny" in Dante Gabriel Rossetti, *Poems,* ed. Oswald Doughty, London, 1957, 63–72, especially ll. 276–97 (I have been unable to obtain the 1911 edition of Rossetti's *Works* edited by William M. Rossetti).

27. De Vane, *Studies in Philology,* 468–69.

28. Rossetti, *Poems,* 258.

29. F. G. Stephens, *The Portfolio,* May 1894, 38.

30. Roman Jakobson, "On the Verbal Art of William Blake and Other Poet-Painters," *Linguistic Inquiry,* I, 1970, 3–23.

31. Surtees, I, 27, No. 64.

32. *William Holman Hunt*, Liverpool, 1969, 35, No. 27. The further Scriptural passages in the R. A. Catalogue of 1854, however, were later disclaimed by Hunt, as Allen Staley kindly informed me.

33. "The River's Record," written in 1871, was published under the title "Down Stream" in the 1881 edition of the *Poems*. See Doughty, 1949, 478.

34. Susan Casteras, "The Double Vision in Portraiture," *Rossetti*, New Haven, 1976, 13.

35. D. G. Rossetti, letter to William Michael Rossetti, 1849, *Letters*, I, 64, No. 47.

36. The drawing for the illustration, now in the Birmingham City Museum and Art Gallery, is published by Surtees, I, No. 83 and II, pl. 108.

37. D. G. Rossetti, *Letters*, I, 74, No. 49.

38. Rossetti's interest in Ingres continued, or revived, in two pencil studies for *The Question of 1875*, a subject clearly inspired by Ingres's *Oedipus and the Sphinx*, which Rossetti may have seen in the Exposition Universelle of 1855 in Paris. For the connection between these late drawings and Ingres's work, see Carl A. Peterson, "Rossetti and the Sphinx," *Apollo*, LXXXV, 1967, 48–53.

39. The lines are cited from the 1849 version of the sonnets "Roger Rescuing Angelica" (see note 36 above). For the version included in the 1870 edition of the *Poems* and there entitled "For 'Ruggiero and Angelica' by Ingres," see Dante Gabriel Rossetti, *Poems*, 1957, 138–39.

40. See Bandelin, *Rossetti*, New Haven, 1976, 45–47.

41. For a related drawing, *The Sonnet* of 1880, and its accompanying sonnet, see *Rossetti*, New Haven, 1976, 103 and No. 55. For a discussion of the lost drawing portraying a winged female figure labeled "Anima" of 1880, see Jane Bayard, " 'Lustral Rites and Dire Portents': Works from 1872 to 1882," ibid., 95.

42. Bayard, *Rossetti*, New Haven, 1976, 97.

43. 31 August 1871. *Letters*, III, 906, No. 1158.

44. "Leyland was here today and seems likely to buy the Blasted Damdozel . . ."; letter to Frederic James Shields, 30 January 1881, *Letters*, IV, 1842, No. 2401. The reference to the "Blowed Damozel" appears in a letter to Ford Madox Brown of May 1873 (*Letters*, III, 1166, No. 1335). For a discussion of Rossetti's artistic demoralization and reference to "Bdy Dam," see Doughty, 1949, 607–8.

45. Letter to Frederick James Shields, 27 August 1869, *Letters*, II, 729, No. 862. The same thought is expressed in a letter to Thomas Gordon Hake of 21 April 1870: "The bread-and-cheese question has led to a good deal of my painting being pot-boiling and no more—whereas my verse, being nonprofitable, has remained (as much as I have found time for) unprostituted" (*Letters*, II, 850, No. 992).

46. 28 May 1873, *Letters*, III, 1175, No. 1345.

47. Surtees, I, 27, No. 64.

48. Cited by Bayard, *Rossetti*, New Haven, 1976, 102.

4

Some Women Realists

Women artists have turned to realism since the nineteenth century, through force of circumstance if not through inclination. Cut off from access to the high realm of History Painting, with its rigorous demands of anatomy and perspective, its idealized classical or religious subjects, its grand scale and its man-sized rewards of prestige and money, women turned to more accessible fields of endeavor: to portraits, still life and genre painting, the depiction of everyday life, realism's chosen arena.

Like the realist novel—another area in which women have been permitted to exercise their talents since the nineteenth century— genre painting, and realist art generally, has been thought to afford a more direct reflection of the woman artist's specifically feminine concerns than abstract or idealized art, because of the accessibility of its language. Yet one must be as wary of reading "feminine" attitudes in, or into, realist works as into abstract paintings. While being a woman—like being an American or being a dwarf or having been born in 1900 rather than in 1940—may be a variable, even an important variable, in the creation of the art work, little can be predicted on its basis. That a given artist is a woman constitutes a necessary but by no means a sufficient condition of her choice of a given style or subject: it is one element along with others, like her nationality, her age, her training, her temperament, her response to available modes of expression, or her priorities of self-identification.

For the woman realist, like the woman artist in general, the sense of the creative self *as* a woman may play a greater or a lesser role in the formulation of pictorial imagery. In the past few years, with the rise of a powerful and articulate women's movement, this sense of conscious feminine identification has become a more dominant factor in the work of many women artists, who have begun to define themselves more concretely *as* women, and to identify their feelings and interests with those of other women in the realms of art and politics, and in their private realms of imagination as well.

It is, of course, difficult to separate unconscious or half-conscious motives from conscious intentions in the choice of a given realist motif or vantage point. Does a woman choose to depict her living-room floor, the Virgin of the Macarena, or mothers and children, rather than trucks, motorcycles, and pinups out of conscious feminist principles, or the promptings of the unconscious, or because such material is familiar to her and easily available, or for a combination of such reasons? To what extent does the depiction of close-up, large-scale views of fruit or flowers, a fairly popular motif among current women realists, depend on some sort of archetypal imprinting of the female psyche, and to what extent on the fact that a major woman artist, Georgia O'Keeffe, made such imagery her trademark? To what degree should realist works be read as iconological symbols—that is, conveyors of unconsciously or semiconsciously held attitudes or ideas and more specifically, as conveyors of unequivocally feminine world views? These issues all come into play in a consideration of the work of some women realists.

1. Social Realists

To a nineteenth-century English genre painter like Emily Mary Osborn, realism (with a small *r*), if she thought about it at all, meant what it did to most of her contemporaries and has continued to mean to most of the public ever since: subject matter from the contemporary world; a tone which is didactic and moralizing; and a style which is clear, representational, and often richly detailed in its delineation of locale, type, and situation.

Osborn surely must be considered a proto-feminist artist: her major works deal with the problems facing the women of her time. *The Governess,* exhibited at the Royal Academy in 1860 and bought by Queen Victoria herself, constituted a bitter pictorial indictment of the "practice of treating educated women as if they were menial servants," to borrow the words of a contemporary reviewer; other works, like *For the Last Time, Half the World Knows Not How the Other Half Lives,* or *God's Acre,* touch on timely issues of poverty and social oppression specifically as they effect the lives of women. Her best-known work, *Nameless and Friendless* (see Figure 9 in Chapter 1), is one of the rare nineteenth-century paintings to deal directly with the lot of the woman artist.

It is a painting that was meant to be read and interpreted rather than to be appreciated for its not inconsiderable visual qualities alone. Such a work necessarily employed some of the strategies of the novel, the theater, or the sociological treatise to achieve its ends, and often seems to prophesy the silent film in its emphasis on accurate, significant detail and meaningful gesture. Yet it is wrong to dismiss such examples of Victorian realism as *Nameless and Friendless* as merely "photographic" or "literary" simply because they do not accord with today's established canons of pictorial decorum. They should, on the contrary, be considered a different but equally legitimate and viable mode of visual structure and expression. While it is richly detailed and full of social and psychological information, a work like *Nameless and Friendless* is paradoxically not at all photographic, in the way the work of many present-day realists may be said to be so. Victorian narrative painting, in the complexity of its organization, the explicitness of its social and moral implications and its dramatically meaningful condensations is at the furthest pole of expression, in its approach to the raw material of experience, from the diffidence and objectivity characteristic of the photographic sensibility. Osborn's work, rather than constituting an apparently random slice through time, like a photographic image, is a carefully constructed palimpsest of significant temporal incidents from which a complex message may be distilled.

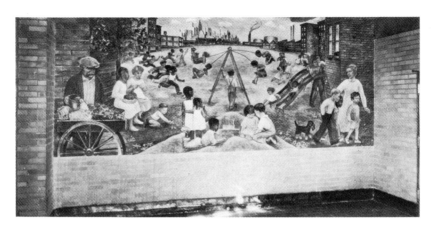

1. Lucienne Bloch. *The Cycle of a Woman's Life.* Mural, Women's House of Detention, New York (now destroyed)

Such a didactic and socially meaningful type of realist expression has had its adherents among women artists of the twentieth century. In our own country, during the 1930s, the art programs of the New Deal offered an opportunity to artists of both sexes to create works which commented on the social issues of the day, and which were located on the walls of those public institutions where their messages might reach an appropriate public. In several cases, women artists working on government-sponsored commissions took the opportunity to comment, in large-scale wall-paintings, on those social issues which particularly concerned women or in which women constituted the critical motif.

Such was the case in Lucienne Bloch's ambitious mural [1], now lost, for the Women's House of Detention in New York, of 1936. Bloch chose a theme relevant to the female audience—the cycle of a woman's life—and placed it in a context familiar to the women prisoners, a city playground in a working-class district. A certain didactic overtone is perceptible in the iconography, in that black and white children mingle and share toys and food while their mothers chat companionably; an unintentionally darker note is struck by the fact that a cityscape of factories, skyscrapers, and gas tanks quite literally closes off the horizon. Bloch was straightforward about her attempt to program social significance and utility into her art: first of all, she felt that the prison context itself created "a crying need for bright colors and bold curves to offset [the] drabness and austerity." Second, she wanted to combat the inmates' suspicion of art "as something highbrow . . . severed from the people and placed upon a pedestal for the privilege of museum students, art patrons and art dealers" by relating her own work to their lives as closely as possible. "Since they were women and for the most part products of poverty and slums, I chose the only subject which would not be foreign to them—children—framed in a New York landscape of the most ordinary kind." Finally, the artist discovered that her actual presence making the mural had a quite concrete, if not traditionally aesthetic, impact on the women inmates: "They wholeheartedly enjoyed watching me paint. The mural was not a foreign thing to them. In fact, in the inmates' make-believe moments, the children in the mural were adopted and named."[1]

The social idealism and public concern of the New Deal even made its impact on such a private and idiosyncratic realist style as that of Florine Stettheimer. Her *Cathedrals of Wall Street* of 1939 (see Figure 5 in Chapter 5), one of a series of cathedrals of New York, is a loving but subversive homage to Eleanor Roosevelt, who occupies the center stage, elegant in Eleanor blue, with Mayor La Guardia dancing attendance and Franklin relegated to inanimate glory as a sort of Pantocrator on the flattened white-and-gold facade of the Stock Exchange, flanked by a gorgeous golden George Washington. This record of democratic pageantry is couched in a language of such lighthearted decorative prolixity that it deftly undermines, at the same time that it reflects, the more pompous and pretentious large-scale monuments of social significance of the time.

Interestingly enough, many of the women artists who choose to comment on the social issues of the day in their art at the present moment—May Stevens comes to mind, or Faith Ringgold—tend to turn to more abstract or decorative pictorial languages, perhaps feeling that social concern or political protest are more forcefully conveyed by symbolic rather than descriptive means today.

2. Evocative Realism

What Cindy Nemser has called "the close-up vision"—"the urge to get up close, to zero in, to examine details and fragments"—has played a major role in the imagery of many contemporary women realists.[2] This kind of realism is at a far remove from the social variety, with its emphasis on the concrete verities of setting and situation.

It was a woman artist, Georgia O'Keeffe, who first severed the minutely depicted object—shell, flower, skull, pelvis—from its moorings in a justifying space or setting, and freed it to exist, vastly magnified, as a surface manifestation of something other (and somehow deeper, both literally and figuratively) than its physical reality on the canvas. One can think of the work of O'Keeffe and of such contemporary painters of relatively large-scaled, centralized, up-front realistic images of fruit, flowers, or seed-pods as Buffie Johnson, Nancy Ellison, or Ruth Gray as "symbolic" in their realism as long as we are very explicit about the nature of the symbolism involved.

O'Keeffe's *Black Iris* of 1927 like Ruth Gray's iris in *Midnight Flower* of 1972, or Nancy Ellison's cut pear in *Opening* of 1970, or Buffie Johnson's *Pomegranate* of 1972, is a hallucinatingly accurate image of a plant form at the same time that it constitutes a striking natural symbol of the female genitalia or reproductive organs. The kind of symbolism implicit to these women's imagery, O'Keeffe's iris, for example, is radically different from that of more traditional symbolism, like the so-called hidden symbolism of the fifteenth-century Flemish realists.[3] In the case of the latter, the depicted object —the "vehicle" of the pictorial metaphor, to borrow a term from literary criticism—refers to some abstract quality, shared by itself and the subject, or "tenor" of the metaphor, which it serves to convey. The irises in the vase in the foreground of Hugo van der Goes's *Portinari Altarpiece*, far from being sexual symbols, refer to the future sorrow of the Virgin at the Passion of Christ. The significance may have been suggested by the notion of the sword-shaped leaves of the flower "piercing the Virgin's heart," an implication made even more obvious in the name of the closely related

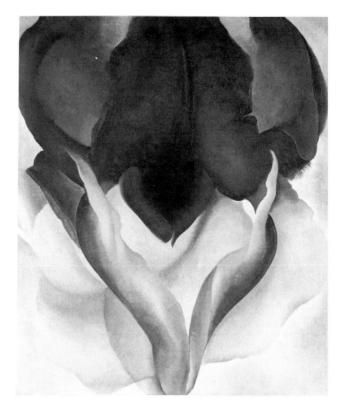

2. Georgia O'Keeffe. *Black Iris*

gladiola, which is derived from the Latin word for sword. But the meaning of the flower is hardly visually self-evident. In the older work, the symbolic relation between the minutely rendered irises and the abstract suffering of the Virgin obviously depends on a shared context of meaning—the iconography of the Nativity: it is something the spectator is supposed to know, not something that strikes him or her the minute he or she sees the flower in its vase.

In O'Keeffe's *Black Iris* [2] or Gray's *Midnight Flower,* on the contrary, the connection "iris-female genitalia" is immediate: it is not so much that one stands for the other, but rather that the two meanings are almost interchangeable. The analogy is based not on a shared abstract quality, but rather upon a morphological similarity between the physical structure of the flower and that of woman's sexual organs—hence on a visual, concrete similarity rather than an abstract, contextually stipulated relation. In the same way, Johnson's pomegranate suggests woman as a fruitful being—it is morphologically similar to the uterus; the richness of female fecundity —the seeds well up from inside the pomegranate; and her reproductive expandability—the fruit splits under the pressure of its own ripeness—without ever being anything other than a carefully observed and described, if large-scale, pomegranate. (The fruit's mythological significance in the story of Proserpine may or may not play a role in the metaphorical significance of the work, but knowledge of the myth is certainly not essential to our response to its other implications.)

Such morphological metaphors were particularly attractive to the Surrealists, for they tend to be apprehended intuitively rather than depending on previous information, to make their appeal on the level of fantasy and imagination, or unconscious association, rather than to the intellect. As such, they lend themselves admirably to that imagery of metamorphosis on which the Surrealists relied to upset the uneasy boundaries between thing and thing, substance and substance, perception and hallucination or dream. Yet neither O'Keeffe's, Johnson's nor Ellison's work can be considered "surreal." Their images are simply realist analogs, suggesting and evoking a feminine content—realist images suspended in a suggestive void. If a contemporary artist puts the iris back into a context, O'Keeffe's suggestive aura still plays its role: an interesting, witty new set of implications accrues to the flower in Carolyn Schock's *The Iris* of 1972. Now the irises, desexed and casual, have been put back into a still-life setting of deliberate artifice, like a studio set-up; but the feminist implications of O'Keeffe's iris as icon are nicely made into a dilemma by situating the vase between a (masculine?) hammer and a (feminine?) fan. The artist has at once desacralized and the same time reactivated the feminist, or feminine, implications of the flower.

3. Literal or Thing-in-Itself Realism

Some women realists today are distinguished precisely because of their choice of unevocative motifs. Artists like Sylvia Mangold, Yvonne Jacquette, Susan Crile, or Janet Fish are really pictorial phenomenologists. In their awareness of the picture surface, their concern with scale, measurement, space or interval, their cool, urban tone, their often assertive and sometimes decorative textures, they tend to affirm the art-work as a literal fact which, while it may have its referent in the actual world, nevertheless achieves its true effectiveness in direct visual experience, not evocation. Certainly, their subjects—floors, windows, ceilings, rugs, jars, bottles—count for something, but for what? Perhaps these are better considered motifs rather than subjects, but with none of the arty overtones that have accrued to this term since the nineteenth century. The images of these painters, neither symbolic, metaphoric, nor suggestive, are, in the rhetoric of pure realism, either metonymic—one thing next to another thing next to another—or synecdochic—a part of something standing for a larger whole.

Janet Fish, with her batallions of jars, honey-pots, glasses, and bottles, traffics in the objecthood of ordinary transparent containers. Their mass-produced curves, their patient, coarse-grained refractions, their elegant or graceless labels are simply there, on the shelf or table. What, after all, can one Coke bottle remind you of besides another Coke bottle? If, in confronting the human figure the realist artist, like certain photographers, as Susan Sontag has recently suggested, somehow violates an implicit moral sanction by cooly transforming human subjects into visual objects, Janet Fish, the painter of glassware or packaged supermarket fruit need face no such accusation. If anything, through over life-sized scale and attentive handling, she confers an unprecedented dignity upon the grouped jelly jars or wine-bottles that she renders with such deference. The glassy fruit- or liquid-filled volumes confront us with the hypnotic solemnity of the processional mosaics at Ravenna, and a similar, faceted, surface sparkle.

Sylvia Mangold, in an oeuvre at once austere and profligate, has devoted herself to exhaustive probing of the phenomenology of the floor: one would guess it is the floor of her own apartment. No photograph would care so much, could be as ostentatiously lavish in its documentation as this dedicated artist; not Walker Evans, not James Agee in his poignant litany to walls and floors and shingles in *Let Us Now Praise Famous Men,* not even Nathalie Sarraute in her thirty-page contemplation of the environs of a doorknob at the beginning of *La Planetarium,* goes farther than Sylvia Mangold in *Floor II.*

"Bareness and space (and spacing) are so difficult and seem to me of such greatness that I shall not even try to write seriously or fully of them," says Agee in *Let Us Now Praise Famous Men* [4]— although of course he has been doing just that all along. Mangold might have said much the same thing, but without the final demur. The floor for Mangold is an absolute, its limits not the horizon but the actual boundaries of the canvas itself. In *Floor with Clothes* this surface is interrupted by the gratuitous spatial markers of dropped clothing: the ordinary, stretched to a hypothetical infinity, is measured by carefully delineated, brutally shapeless, exquisitely individuated cast-offs.

In 1968, when Mangold created *Floor II* [3] within the context of dominant hard-edge abstraction, color-field, and Pop, what did it mean to paint a floor with methodical seriousness—straight? What was—and is—the significance of such a choice (*not such a subject*), of such a procedure? While the painting may look simple, the reasons for its being the way it is or for its being at all are probably not. It is both related to, and yet at the same time constitutes a subversion of, the abstract art of the time. Of course, the very existence of nonrelational abstraction gave the artist permission to consider something as neutral as a stretch of floor a plausible motif. But if *Floor II* is at once absolutely pure of conventional meaning or "content," like an abstract motif, at the same time it is a representation of an irrevocably concrete *gegeben* out there: it is appropriation, not invention. *Floor*'s challenge of abstraction is vividly demonstrated by the identification of the *recession* of the floor with the *surface* of the canvas. Are we looking through or at the picture plane? And from where?

Mangold's mode of approach is a detachment so passionate that,

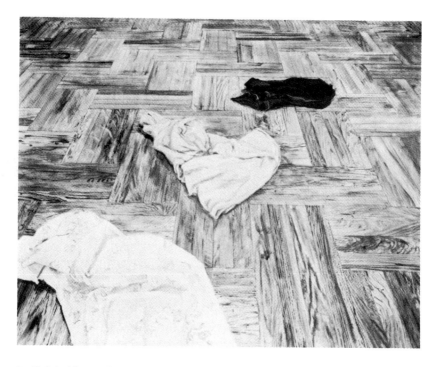

3. Sylvia Mangold. *Floor II*

taken as a state of mind, it might well be considered obsession. Her mood may find antecedents in the methodological obsessiveness of certain Surrealists like Ernst in his wood-grain *frottages* or Magritte in that deadpan literalism of texture particularly characteristic of his wood surfaces. But the Surrealists' textural obsessions were always located in a supportive setting of ambiguity or hysteria: they were not simply direct statements of how it is if you look down at the living-room floor for a long time, with or without the help of a photograph. Very sixties perhaps, is that sense of an intensely personal vantage point which is at the same time very cool and noncommittal. If *Floor II* is anti-poetic and anti-evocative, yet it is a reminder that there is such a thing as a deliberately anti-poetic poetry, and that the innovative force of the French New Novel, which tried to use prose to erase its own significance, reached its zenith in the sixties. The extraordinarily muted yet rapier-sharp realist imagery of an artist like Vija Celmins offers, perhaps, the best parallel with Robbe-Grillet's attempt to abolish significance in literature: is her *Eraser* of 1970 a sly reference to the French writer's *Les Gommes*, as well as being a self-evident Pink Pearl by Eberhard Faber and nothing more?

Nothing but what is, the thing in itself: that seems to be what Mangold is after. Floors have always been *in* paintings. Jan van Eyck and Ingres seem to have enjoyed them, and the nineteenth-century realist Gustave Caillebotte, was positively gaga about one in his prophetically literal, high-horizoned *Floor-Scrapers* of 1875, but they have always been a background incident in the work, not, as in Mangold's paintings, the whole subject of it.

But, by implication, Mangold's floor must be part of a larger whole, too: the orthogonals must meet somewhere. The feminine variable, a single strand in the weaving together of possible intentions and motivations, may be worth considering in this larger context, the world beyond the floor. If a woman is hemmed in by the domestic scene, if floors, toys, and laundry are her daily fare, she can still turn adversity into advantage, constructing out of the meanest, most neglected aspects of experience an imagery horizonless and claustrophobic, yes, but concrete, present, unchallengeable in its verisimilitude. The very mode of approach—part by part, methodical, a little at a time, like folding the laundry, like knitting, like *cleaning* a floor very very carefully, as opposed, say, to the explosive spontaneity, the all-over conquest of a Pollock—has its roots in a social reality. Someone said of Chardin in the eighteenth century: "Nothing humiliates his brush"; in the twentieth century we have to go farther to search out that nothing, and it is *her* brush that is not humiliated; or perhaps creates a triumph of self-imposed humility.

Yvonne Jacquette did a floor, *The James Bond Car Painting*, in 1967. Here, the domestic vantage point is more explicitly spelled out, the dimensions of quotidian reality measured by an overflowing wastebasket, the bottom of a desk, the foot of a music stand, a toy train, and the James Bond car itself. The painting was part of a series concerning space between objects, according to the artist, and this issue of spaces between things has continued to inspire Jacquette in an art of greater range but perhaps less intensity than that of Mangold. For Jacquette, space is a function of glimpses—up, out, down, around—of clouds through windows, of light fixtures on ceilings, of a fraction of shingled barn against the sky. This is not the movement-suggesting Impressionist glimpse of the fleeting moment, but the casting of a colder, more fixative eye. Once again, one is tempted to view these diffident cut-off views as synecdoches pointing to a larger whole: women may be stuck with glimpses for their visual nourishment, yet the pictorial tensions generated by the interplay between space and the things that interrupt its freedom are, after all, what makes art interesting or what makes art art; and this is the case whether the space in question is the living-room floor and the interruption the children's toys, or the Sistine Ceiling and the interruption the hand of God.

4. Painters of the Figure

That fear of content, of the transgression of experienced reality into the *hortus conclusus* of the image, which has marked the most extreme phases of the modern movement in recent years, is at least in part responsible for the demise of the portrait as a respectable field of specialization. That is not to say that advanced artists of the twentieth century have not tried their hands at this time-honored genre: there is Picasso's portrait of Gertrude Stein, Kokoschka's of Dr. Tietze and his wife, or Matisse's of Mlle Landsberg, to name only a few. In the last few years, realists like Alex Katz, Philip Pearlstein, and Chuck Close have helped revive the genre; and of course, photographic portraits have always been accepted, indeed, at times, encouraged, as somehow appropriate for a mechanical medium rather than a truly creative one like painting. Yet there is surely nothing to compare, in the twentieth century, with the enormous and inventive achievement of major portraitists of the past, like Rembrandt, Hals, or Velázquez, who devoted their best efforts to the field. Even in the nineteenth century, a self-appointed custodian of the grand tradition like Ingres exhibited a haughty reluctance to waste the valuable time he might have been devoting to history painting on mere portraiture, despite the fact that high society was willing to pay well for the privilege.[5] And while it is quite true that the Impressionists and Post-Impressionists were highly responsive to the visual appearance of the contemporary world in the shape of their own circle of family and friends, on the one hand, and to the claims of intensified response to human subjects on the other, it is equally true that the modernist attitude to such works has been to play down their status as portraits and to emphasize the formal inventiveness of paintings like Manet's *Zola*, van Gogh's *Woman of Arles (Mme Ginoux)*, and Cézanne's *Vollard*, as though there were some necessary contradiction between responsiveness to the picture plane and to human character. In short, one might say that portrait painting has been peripheral to the central concerns of much of the advanced art of our times.

In the field of portraiture, women have been active among the subverters of the natural laws of modernism. This hardly seems accidental: women have, after all, been encouraged, if not coerced, into making responsiveness to the moods, attentiveness to the character traits (and not always the most attractive ones) of others into a lifetime's occupation. What is more natural than that they should put their subtle talents as seismographic recorders of social position, as quivering reactors to the most minimal subsurface psychological tremors, to good use in their art? For the portrait is implicated, to some degree at least—whether artist, sitter, or critic wish to admit it or not—in "that terrible need for contact" to which Katherine Mansfield makes such poignant reference in the pages of her *Journal*. Unlike any other genre, the portrait demands the meeting of two subjectivities: if the artist watches, judges the sitter, the sitter is privileged, by the portrait relation, to watch and judge back. In no other case does *what* the artist is painting exist on the same plane of freedom and ontological equality as the artist her or himself, and in no other case is the role of the artist as *mediator* rather than dictator or inventor so literally accentuated by the actual situation in which the art work comes into being. This is particularly true of the representations or relatives, friends, or kindred spirits—rather than commissions—and of course, of self-portrayal—characteristic of the best twentieth-century portraiture.

The number of women painters for whom the portrait and self-portrait have been important, or even major, concerns within the last hundred years is large, even if we exclude highly competent professional specialists in portrait commissions like Cecilia Beaux: their ranks include such artists as Mary Cassatt, Paula Modersohn-Becker, Romaine Brooks, Florine Stettheimer, and, in more recent years, a woman who has devoted an entire oeuvre of great variety and inventiveness almost exclusively to the portrait: Alice Neel. Neel is just now coming into her own after forty years of painting, with a retrospective at the Whitney Museum and several magazine articles, the most important of which, by Cindy Nemser, however, appeared—significantly enough—*not* in an art journal but in the feminist publication *Ms.* [6] Why, one wonders, was Neel for so long refused serious consideration, or, even more insidiously, was her work relegated to consideration as the pictorial equivalent of *vers de société,* her achievement equated with skillful social satire, always with the implication that "real" art had better things to do? (One remembers, of course, that Manet was regretfully written off by his academic teacher Couture as "nothing more than the Daumier of his times.") Neel's portraits, far from being merely witty or clever—although to be so is itself no mean achievement—form a consistent, serious, and innovative body of work: she has, progressively over the years, invented an idiosyncratic structure of line, color, and composition to body forth her vision of unmistakably contemporary character. Twenty or thirty years hence, looking back at the exposed thighs, the patent leather polyphony of the shoes, the world-weary individualism of the *Gruen Family* (1970) or the casual yet somehow startling *rapprochement* of self-exposure and self-containment—of pose, color scheme, and personality—achieved in *Gregory Battcock and David Bourdon* (1971), we will be forced to admit, sighing, blushing or wincing as the case may be, "so *that's* the way we were!"

One thinks of van Gogh's Neunen period portraits of peasants, weavers, railway workers and also of his intention to be an "illustrator of the people" when confronted by the dark, brooding, unrelenting, intensities of Neel's early representations of the people of Spanish Harlem, where she lived during the forties. There is the same deliberate brutalizing of the means to achieve more penetrating

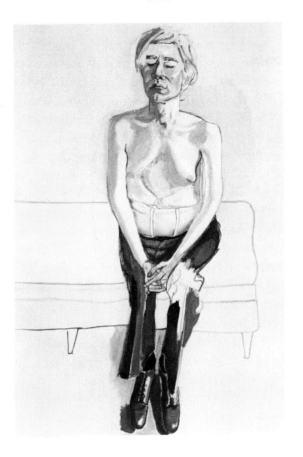

4. Alice Neel. *Andy Warhol*

pictorial ends, the same refusal to rely upon stereotype or sentimentality, the same inability to patronize one's subjects or to see them as mere picturesque generalizations for the human condition. Neel's later works, too, like *Dorothy Pearlstein* of 1969, *Vera Beckerhoff* of 1972, or *Nancy and Her Baby* of 1967 may also call to mind precedents by van Gogh: the single portraits recall the stiff, dignified, almost *Épinal* awkwardness of his *Postman Roulin;* the mother and child his *Mother Roulin and Her Baby* with its disquieting interlacing of maternal and childish forms. Facing the terrible portrait of *Andy Warhol* [4], livid, bandaged, trussed, sewn, and scarred, visibly dropping yet willing himself to a ghastly modicum of decorum after his

UNIVERSITY COLLEGE LIBRARY SWANSEA

near-assassination, one is reminded somehow of van Gogh's intention, in painting the melancholy Dr. Gachet, to record "the heart broken expression of our time." There is no question of derivativeness in any of her work: it is simply a fact that few of her subjects have escaped the inroads of contemporary anxiety—a peculiarly New York brand of it—each, of course, in his or her own particular fashion. Nobody is ever quite relaxed in a Neel portrait, no matter how suggestive of relaxation the pose: some quivering or crisping of the fingers, some devouring patch of shadow under the eyes or insidious wrinkle beneath the chin, a linear quirk, a strategic if unexpected foreshortening dooms each sitter-victim to premonitory alertness as though in the face of impending menace.

This lurking uneasiness is not something Neel reads into her sitters; rather, it has to do with her peculiar phenomenology of the human situation. It is how Neel sees us, how we actually exist for her, and so it is there. Or rather, at times, she doesn't so much *see* it that way as record it, in the same way that Courbet once, without realizing what he was painting, is said to have recorded a distant heap of faggots by simply putting down what he saw until the paint strokes revealed themselves to be what they were. Recently, when I was sitting for her, Neel said to me, "You know, you don't *seem* so anxious, but that's how you come out," genuinely puzzled. Of course, one might say that a person's exterior, if it is keenly enough explored and recorded with sufficient probity, will ultimately give up the protective strategies devised by the sitter for facing the world. Neel felt genuine regret, perhaps, that this was the case; nevertheless, since it was, to paint otherwise would have been merely flattering rather than truthful.

The nude portrait is a subcategory of portraiture that seems to have appealed to certain women artists perhaps because of the subversive nature of the contradiction it implies: the generalization of the nude juxtaposed with the specificity of the portrait. This jarring conjunction was perhaps, as the art historian Eunice Lipton has suggested, a significant factor in the hostility aroused by Manet's *Olympia* when it was shown in Paris more than a hundred years ago. The nude—even cubist or surrealist—is somehow supposed to be timeless, ageless, and, above all, anonymous, not someone you might meet on the street, shake hands with, or bump into at a cocktail party. Here again, Neel has challenged tradition, both old and new, not least in choosing male nudes as her subjects. As early as 1933, she portrayed a frontal and thrice-endowed Joe Gould, recognizable in every respect, and more recently a no less totally individuated John Perrault, languid and hairy, stretched out on a couch. Neel's nude portraits of pregnant women are particularly incisive: the reclining *Pregnant Woman* of 1971, with her ballooning, brown-lined belly and distended nipples, but also the less well-known but no less interesting seated *Pregnant Betty* of 1968. In the latter portrait, the subject, although naked, is firmly rooted in a precise time and place both by her own stylishness and the artist's style, as well as by the exactly recorded, extreme, degree of her pregnancy. No rhetorical generalizations are predicated upon the sitter's condition. Neel has deliberately contraverted the primitive or archetypal clichés associated with incipient motherhood—earth mother or fertility goddess—by dwelling on its very *unnaturalness* for this sophisticated, individuated, urban woman. She plays the force of the temporarily swollen, turgid, bulging breasts and belly (nature's realm) against the fashionable delicacy of the arms and legs, the up-to-dateness of the ravaged coiffure, the painted artifice of makeup and toenail polish, welding these contradictions into an uneasy union predicated upon self-exposure, discomfort, and a wary isolation, defiantly unassimilable to the comforting mystique of childbearing.

Exposure, or self-exposure, has surely been one of the chief motivations behind an even more specialized subcategory of portraiture: the nude, or partially nude, self-portrait. An element of masochism, defiance and self-humiliation at once, seems implicit in the male artist's literally "bearing his breast"—and even more—to the public. In the case of female artists, the implications of the nude self-portrait are quite different. While we are culturally conditioned to expect the *subject* of a self-portrait to be male, we do not expect him to be nude; in the case of a woman, our expectations are reversed: while we certainly expect her to be *nude*, we do not expect her to be the subject of a self-portrait. (How many "Portraits of the Artist as a Young Woman" can one readily call to mind?) Paula Modersohn-Becker led the way with her delicate yet powerful nude

Self-Portrait of 1906, in which the paradisiacal felicities of Gauguin's exotic Eves or Liliths are called into question by the brooding Teutonic seriousness of the flower-wreathed head, the weary sag of the heavy shoulders. More recently, Jane Kogan has posed for herself in an equally paradisiac if far more provocative situation in her *Interiorized Self-Portrait*. Here, the artist's aggressively womanly body merges with and emerges from an equally aggressively mannish suit; her head-on, spectacled glance is shaded by a no-nonsense derby; and she grasps a flower in one hand and a cat-o-nine-tails in the other.

A still further refinement on the nude, female self-portrait theme is the double portrait in which the female member of the pair rather than the male (one might think of *Rembrandt* and *Saskia* as the more traditional prototype) is the artist, and the male is reduced—or elevated, depending on how one looks at it—to the role of compan-

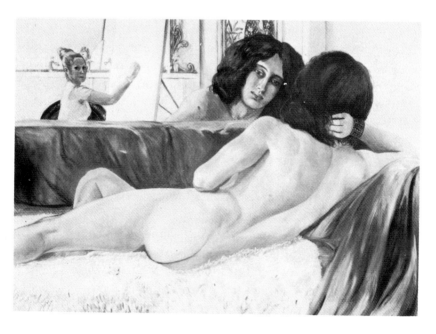

5. Sylvia Sleigh. *Philip Golub Reclining*

ion-model. Sylvia Sleigh made this sex-role reversal quite explicit in her *Philip Golub Reclining* [5] of 1972, where she represents herself as the clothed, active artist, in the process of recording the nude, passive, male model before her. Quite different in mood but similar in its pictorial reversal of customary expectations is Marcia Marcus's *Double Portrait I* of 1972–73. The artist has represented herself standing before the Lion Gates of Mycenae, alert and self-contained, clad in a transparent nightgown; potential energy is suggested by the crinkly expansiveness of her hair, its linear tensions reiterated by the intricacy of the lace insert over her breasts. Her figure is backed up by the towering, masculine yet gently drooping image of a tender, fair-haired flower child, whose brilliantly patterned pants evoke the innocent world of Gauguin's islanders, and whose eyes are exactly the same pristine shade of blue as the Greek sky in the background.

It is Sylvia Sleigh, perhaps, who most pointedly raises the issues involved in the female artist's representation of the male nude. While not overtly political in intention, works like her *Nude Portrait of Allan Robinson* (1968), *Paul Rosano Seated, Nude* (1973), *Nick Tischler Nude* (1973), as well as her large-scale group compositions like *The Court of Pan (After Signorelli)* (1973) or *The Turkish Bath* (1973) are certainly political in effect, if we accept sexuality as one of the major political arenas of our day. It seems apparent that many of the ostensibly *formal* criticisms leveled at Sleigh's work—"awkward" or weak drawing, too loose or too tight brushwork, "incorrect" or "labored" perspective, "mechanical" or "disjointed" composition, etc.—are actually reactions to the underlying political implications of her work: her male nudes force a questioning of what is "natural," "acceptable," or "correct" in the realm of feeling or being, as well as in the realm of art. Similar accusations of formal weakness, technical insufficiency, or even willful distortion were, of course, leveled at Courbet, Manet, and even at the young Ingres, at least in part because the underlying politics of their art affronted "normal"—i.e. unconscious or ideological—expectations.

"Both celebratory and ironic," in the words of Leon Golub, father of one of Sleigh's favorite young models, these nudes suggest that to a contemporary woman painter, male nudity need be no more heroic, no less voluptuous than the female variety. The problem of gentling the male without destroying his—at least potential —potency is connected with the difficulty of creating an up-to-date imagery of male sensuality with a predominantly female audience in mind. Individuation is perhaps the key to Sleigh's response to this problem. She, like Martha Edelheit, another interesting painter of male nudes, refuses to consider her naked subjects as anonymous models. Sleigh's male nudes are all portraits, and, so to speak, portraits all the way, down to the most idiosyncratic details of skin tone, configuration of genitalia or body-hair pattern. (Sleigh has stated that her interest in male fur and its infinite variety, while partly due to delight in its sheer decorative possibilities, was also determined by a reaction against the idealizing depilation of the nude body decreed by the academic training of her youth.)

As did Manet in his *Olympia* or his *Déjeuner sur l'herbe*, Sleigh often relates her nudes to the Great Tradition, both as an assertion of continuity in scope and ambition, and, at the same time, as a witty and ironic reminder of values that have been rejected, or in her case, deliberately stood on their heads. At the same time, her reinterpretations of traditionally female nude group scenes, like *The Turkish Bath*, permit her to carry her responsiveness to the generic appeal of male sensuality and, at the same time to each man's distinctive type of physical or psychological attractiveness, to its ultimate pictorial fulfillment. In this large painting, freely based on prototypes by Delacroix and Ingres, the wonderful pink and blond tenderness of Lawrence Alloway's recumbent form is played against the piercing blue intelligence of his glance, and his horizontal image against the swarthy, svelte, romantically aquiline verticality of the adjacent figure of Paul Rosano. In the same fashion, the richly hair-patterned torso of the dreamily relaxed John Perreault is nicely paired off with the stiffer, more frontal glabrousness of that of Scott Burton kneeling beside him, and the delights of these contrasts themselves are set off by the richness and coloristic brilliance of the decorative patterns against or upon which they are set.

The ironies of her work of course reveal the reality of the sexual situation. If we compare Sleigh's male harem scene with Ingres's *Turkish Bath* we see that she has actually dignified her male sitters by stipulating through portrait heads and distinctive physiques that they are differentiable human beings. The faces of Ingres's women are as close to being bodies as they can possibly be without suffering a complete metamorphosis, like Magritte's body-head in *Rape:* they are as devoid of intelligence or energy as breasts or buttocks. This depersonalization is a prime strategy of what Susan Sontag has called the pornographic imagination; indeed, a token of its success in sexualizing all aspects of experience and rejecting anything that might divert from this single-minded goal. Sleigh's wit is at once a weapon and a token of her humanity: instead of annihilating individuality, she evisions it as an essential component of erotic response: instead of depersonalizing the heads of her sitters, she not only accepts their uniqueness but goes still further and intensifies the uniqueness of their bodies as well.

It is an interesting commentary on the inextricability of moral or political judgments from aesthetic ones that so many female observers of Sleigh's paintings experience them as successful, and pictorially accomplished, the subjects as sensually appealing and physically attractive—rather in the same terms that art historians or critics, generally male or trained by men, have responded to the overt erotic appeal of nudes by Watteau, Goya, or Ingres—whereas heterosexual males are often turned off by her works. The latter feel that the figures are "effeminate," the tone "campy," the drawing "weak," "distorted," or "incorrect," perhaps trying to dissociate themselves from what might be a threatening reversal of the power structure, or to rationalize their quite genuine distress and anger about being turned into languid creatures of the bedroom rather than active, privileged visual consumers of centuries of aesthetically certified erotic art products. The liberties taken with the female figure by male artists have always been justified on the grounds of the increased aesthetic and sensual pleasure afforded by such deviations from current canons of academic correctness. Donald Posner, for example, in his recent study of Watteau's nude *Lady at Her Toilet*, counters eighteenth-century criticism of the anatomical deficiencies of Watteau's drawings for this work by admitting that, while such criticisms are not wholly unfair, they are completely beside the point "because the drawings do not aim to articulate the structure and mechanics of bone and muscle, but attempt to capture the voluptuousness of the female body as it surrenders to relaxation, stretches and turns, or curls itself up. In achieving this, these sketches are unsurpassed."[7] Change the adjective before "body" to "male" and one sees the point of Sleigh's interpretation of the nude male form. While the canons of drawing, or of artistic quality, seem quite properly to be relatively flexible and determined by quite specifiable goals or situations, the ideological contexts in which these judgments of quality are formulated, since they are generally hidden or unconscious, are far less amenable to change, or even to rational consideration. The imagery of contemporary women realists like Neel, Sleigh, and many others may demand that we raise these ideological assumptions to the level of conscious attention and face the larger implications of what have previously seemed to be purely aesthetic questions of quality.

Notes

1. Lucienne Bloch, "Murals for Use" in Francis V. O'Connor (ed.), *Art for the Millions: Essays from the 1930's by Artists and Administrators of the WPA Federal Art Project* (Greenwich, Conn.: New York Graphic Society, 1973), pp. 76–77.

2. Cindy Nemser, "The Close-Up Vision—Representational Art, Part II," *Arts Magazine* (May 1972): 44.

3. See Goran Hermeren, *Representation and Meaning in the Visual Arts*, Lund, 1969 (Lund Studies in Philosophy, I), pp. 77–101, for an excellent discussion of iconographical symbolism, including the hidden variety.

4. James Agee and Walker Evans, *Let Us Now Praise Famous Men* (Boston: Houghton Mifflin, 1960; orig. publ. 1939 and 1940), p. 55.

5. Robert Rosenblum, *Jean-Auguste-Dominique Ingres* (New York: Harry N. Abrams, 1967), p. 33.

6. Cindy Nemser, "Alice Neel: Portraits of Four Decades," *Ms.*, October 1973, pp. 48–53.

7. Donald Posner, *Watteau: A Lady at Her Toilet* (Art in Context) (New York: Viking), p. 62.

5

Florine Stettheimer: Rococo Subversive

It is admittedly difficult to reconcile the style and subject matter of Florine Stettheimer with conventional notions of a socially conscious art.[1] The Stettheimer style is gossamer light, highly artificed and complex; the iconography, refined, recondite, and personal in its references. In one of her best known works, *Family Portrait No. 2* [1] of 1933, we see the artist in her preferred setting: New York, West Side, feminine, floral, familial. The family group includes her sister Ettie, whom she had portrayed in an equally memorable individual portrait ten years earlier, sitting to the artist's right. Ettie was a philosopher who had earned a doctorate in Germany with a thesis on William James, but later turned to fiction. She wrote two highly wrought novels, *Philosophy* and *Love Days*, publishing under the pseudonym "Henrie Waste,"[2] novels which would certainly by today's standards be considered feminist in their insistence that woman's self-realization is incompatible with romantic love, and, in the case of *Love Days*, in the demonstration of the devastating results of the wrong sort of amorous attachment.

To the far right is her sister, Carrie, also subject of an earlier individual portrait, hostess of the family parties and creator of the dollhouse now in the Museum of the City of New York. This last

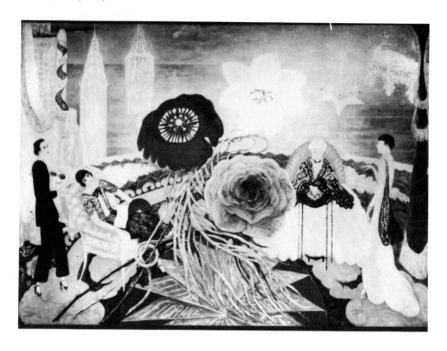

1. Florine Stettheimer. *Family Portrait No. 2*

project was the work of a lifetime, complete with miniature reproductions of masterpieces by such artist-friends of the Stettheimers
as Gaston Lachaise and William and Marguerite Zorach, as well as
a thumbnail version by Marcel Duchamp of his *Nude Descending a
Staircase.* Off center, hieratically enshrined in a shell-like golden
mandorla, is the matriarch, Rosetta Walter Stettheimer. She is here
shawled in lace, Florine's favorite fabric, which Ettie and Carrie are
wearing as well.[3] The artist herself, however, is clad in the dark
painting suit that served as her work outfit, although this relatively
sober turn-out is here set off by sprightly red high-heeled sandals.
The whole world of the Stettheimers, set aloft amid Manhattan's
significant spires, with the blue waters surrounding the island visible
below, is guarded by a stellar Statue of Liberty and domesticated by
the exuberant baldachin of 182 West 58th Street (the Alwyn Court,
their dwelling place). The scene is at once distanced and brought
to the surface of the canvas by the resplendent three-part bouquet

that dominates the composition. Perhaps each flower is meant as a reference to a sister; perhaps the willow-like frond binding them all together is meant to refer to their mother.[4] In any case, the stylish floral life of the bouquet dwarfs and overpowers the human life in the painting. One may choose to see that bouquet, and indeed, the painting as a whole, as a kind of testimonial offered by the artist to her family, her city, and to the very world of vivid artifice she created with them. "My attitude is one of Love/is all adoration/for all the fringes/all the color/all tinsel creation," she wrote.[5]

Certainly the mature style of Florine Stettheimer is based on highly idiosyncratic responses to a wide variety of sources, ranging from the later effusions of Symbolism (including the American variety recently brought to focus by Charles Eldredge in an exhibition at the Grey Gallery) to the decorative style of Henri Matisse and the set designs of the Russian Ballet—projects by Bakst, Benois, and Goncharova—which the artist encountered in Paris before World War I. More specifically, she seems to have been influenced by her friend Adolfo Best-Maugard, the Mexican artist and theorist, who playfully juggles the seven basic forms of his esthetic system in his hand in Stettheimer's 1920 portrait of him. Best-Maugard's *A Method of Creative Design*, first published in 1926, systematizes various vanguard notions of the time into decorative, linear, at times quite witty configurations. His illustrations to the book—"Curtains," "Rosettes and Flowers," or "Modern Surroundings" [2], for example—share many characteristics of Stettheimer's treatment of the same themes, yet can hardly be considered a unique source. On the contrary: Stettheimer had acquired a thorough knowledge of the European art tradition during her years on the Continent; as a student abroad, she had commented on artists, art work and collections at considerable length and often with great astuteness in the pages of her diary.[6] At the same time, she was well aware of the most advanced currents of the art of her own period, and was closely allied through friendship and mutual interest with the people who made it. The Stettheimers' circle of friends included Marcel Duchamp, whose portrait Florine painted in 1923, Elie Nadelman, Albert Gleizes, Gaston Lachaise, William and Marguerite Zorach, and many others. Primitive and folk art seem to have played a role in

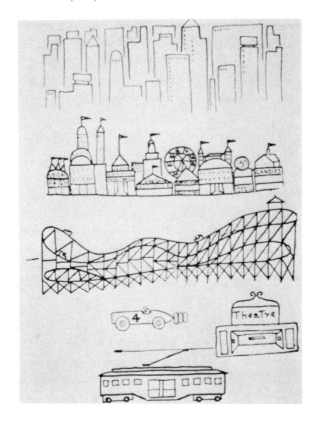

2. Adolfo Best-Maugard. "Modern Surroundings,"
from *A Method of Creative Design*

the formation of the artist's style as well—as did, perhaps, the elegant and incisive graphic stylishness of contemporary *Vanity Fair* cartoons. A comparison of Stettheimer's *Natatorium Undine* of 1927 and *Divers, Divers,* a cartoon of the same year by the witty and feminine Fish,[7] gives some indication of just how far-ranging Stettheimer's eye actually was.

Often, just when we think she is being her most naïvely "uninfluenced," Stettheimer is in fact translating some recherché source into her own idiom. Such is the case with the *Portrait of Myself* of 1923 [3], which draws upon the eccentric and visionary art of William Blake, whose reversal of natural scale, androgynous figure style, and

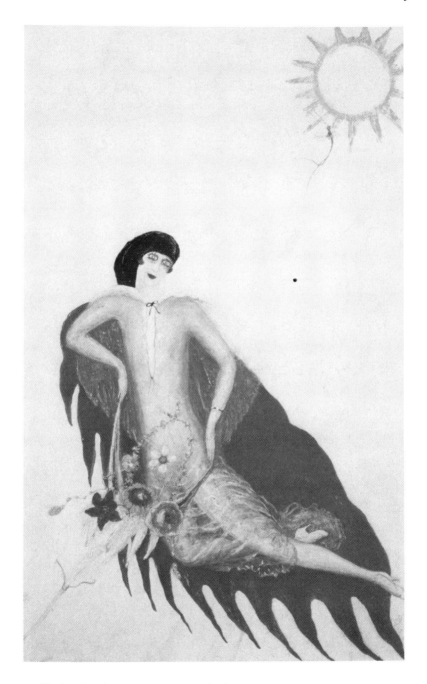

3. Florine Stettheimer. *Portrait of Myself*

intensified drawing seem to have stirred a responsive chord in Stettheimer's imagination. Blake's illustration for his *Song of Los*, with the figure reclining weightlessly on a flower, seems to have been the prototype for Stettheimer's memorable self-portrait, and indeed it had been published in Laurence Binyon's *Drawings and Engravings of William Blake* in 1922. Certainly, the artist was conversant with the literature of art: "I think she must have read everything concerning art published in English, French and German . . . ," wrote her sister Ettie in the introduction to Florine's posthumously published poems in 1949.[8]

But as much as Stettheimer's evolved style depends on resourceful borrowing and translation, even more does it depend, like all original styles, on a good deal of forceful rejection. In order to arrive at her own idiosyncratic language of form, she had to turn away not only from traditional formal values like those embodied in the academic nudes she painted around the turn of the century (while studying with Kenyon Cox at the Art Students' League), but also those of modernist abstraction. In any case, no matter what its derivations or its novelties, Stettheimer's style, at first glance, hardly seems an appropriate vehicle for the rhetoric of social message.

Nor do the subjects of many of the artist's more "documentary" works, like *Studio Party* of 1915 or *Sunday Afternoon in the Country* of 1917, seem to have that public character, that easy accessibility characteristic of a public art of social consciousness. The social character of these works is of a very private kind. The sitters are the privileged denizens of a most exclusive world, the world of the Stettheimers' entertainments, soirées and picnics. In *Studio Party*, along with Florine herself, that world is seen to include the Lachaises, Albert Gleizes, Avery Hopwood, and Leo Stein; in *Sunday Afternoon*, those enjoying themselves in the elaborately cultivated garden of André Brook, the Stettheimers' place in the country, are Marcel Duchamp, Edward Steichen, Adolph Bolm, the dancer, and Jo Davidson, the sculptor. And—an additional touch of esthetic distancing—Stettheimer herself seems to have seen these gatherings as justified by her transformation of them into works of art. In a poem of about 1917, recorded in her diary and later published in

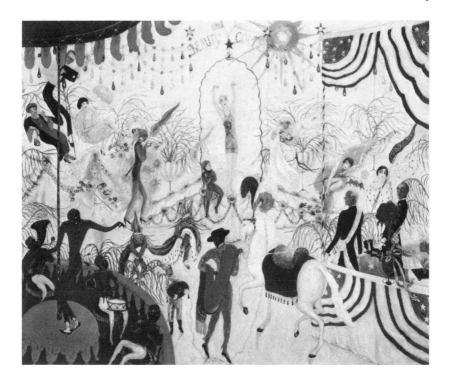

4. Florine Stettheimer. *Beauty Contest*

Crystal Flowers, she says: "Our Parties/Our Picnics/Our Banquets/ Our Friends/ Have at last—a raison d'être/Seen in color and design/ It amuses me/ To recreate them/ To paint them."[9]

Indeed, far from looking like an art of social purpose, Stettheimer's paintings seem as though they might best be considered an expression of Camp sensibility at its highest—the figures weightless, sinuous and androgynous; the settings unswervingly theatrical; the inherent populism or even vulgarity of some subjects, like *Beauty Contest*[10] of 1924 [4] or *Spring Sale at Bendel's* of 1922, mediated by a pictorial structure fantastically rococo, distanced by decorative reiteration. And Camp sensibility, defined by Susan Sontag in her seminal article of 1964 as "a certain mode of aestheticism," of seeing the world in terms of a degree of artifice, of stylization[11] (a definition which serves admirably to sum up Stettheimer's pictorial expression), is explicitly contrasted by Sontag with artistic attitudes of deep social concern and awareness. She sees Camp sensibility as opposing both the moralism of high culture and the tension between moral and esthetic passion which she finds characteristic of avant-garde art; it is, in her phrase, "wholly aesthetic."[12] "It goes without saying," she asserts, "that the Camp sensibility is disengaged, depoliticized—or at least apolitical."[13]

Yet in insisting on the explicitly *social* impulse behind Stettheimer's art while pointing out its overtly Camp qualities, I am not being merely paradoxical. Rather, it seems to me that events and shifts of ideological position in the more than fifteen years since "Notes on 'Camp'" appeared—above all, that striking redefinition of what is generally considered to be social and political in import rather than private or even esthetic, a change effected largely by public and militant activism of blacks, women, and gays (the very territory of Camp itself, from *Prancing Nigger* to the present)—have made us far more aware of an actively subversive component inherent to Camp sensibility itself. This subversiveness may be quite validly viewed as social or political commitment in its own right.

In 1980, there is justification for seeing Camp—in many ways a fiercer and more self-assured continuation of the half-petulant, half-parodic foot-stamping poses of fin-de-siècle Decadence—as a kind of permanent revolution of self-mocking sensibility against the strictures of a patriarchal tradition and the solemn, formalist teleology of vanguardism. This recent transformation of the ideological implications of Camp is itself a good reason for taking seriously a notion like that of the "social consciousness" of Stettheimer.

When we get down to looking at the artist and her work concretely and in detail, however, we might do better to view her reconciliation of social awareness and a highly wrought Camp vision of life as simply one of a number of paradoxes inherent to her nature and her situation. First of all, Stettheimer was both an insider and an outsider: comfortably wealthy, a giver of parties, a friend of many interesting and famous people, but Jewish (and, as the pages of her diary reveal, very aware of it) and, although an artist, a very private artist, known only to a rather special group of admirers, and a woman artist at that. Secondly, she was a determined feminist, yet equally determined to be feminine in the most conventional sense of the term: her bedroom was a dream-construction of lace and cellophane, her clothing and demeanor ladylike; yet at the same time, she was capable of voicing in her poetry a quite outspoken and prickly antagonism toward male domination. One such poem, published in the posthumous volume of her verse, *Crystal Flowers,* is an ironic musing on models: "Must one have models/ must one have models forever/ nude ones/ draped ones/ costumed ones/ 'The Blue Hat'/ 'The Yellow Shawl'/ 'The Patent Leather Slippers'/ Possibly men painters really/ need them—they created them."[14] Still another, titled "To a Gentleman Friend," begins, quite startlingly: "You fooled me you little floating worm . . .";[15] while another, more poignant and untitled, sums up bitterly the self-muting deception forced on women by the men who admire them: "Occasionally/ A human being/ Saw my light/ Rushed in/ Got singed/ Got scared/ Rushed out/ Called fire/ Or it happened/ That he tried/ To subdue it/ Or it happened/ He tried to extinguish it/ Never did a friend/ Enjoy it/ The way it was/ So I learned to/ Turn it low/ Turn it out/ When I meet a stranger—/ Out of courtesy/ I turn on a soft/ Pink light/ Which is found modest/ Even charming/ It is a protection/ Against wear/ And tears/ And when/ I am rid of/ The Always-to-be-Stranger/ I turn on my light/ And become myself."[16]

Self-contradictions abound in the Stettheimer personality and outlook. She was a snob but an ardent New Dealer, a fanatic party-giver who in her diary complained of a particularly spectacular party given in her honor that "it was enough to make a socialist of any human being with a mind." Some of these contradictory stances are admittedly trivial; others are less paradoxical than they seem. For a woman, for instance, the boundaries between subjective preoccupation and social awareness are by no means absolute; at times they effectively coincide. Then again, both the snob and the social activist share a highly developed sensitivity to the defining characteristics of class and milieu. And finally, and perhaps most important in separating apparent contradiction from the real variety, although Florine Stettheimer may have gloried in *artifice*—that is to say, the authentic and deliberate creation of fantasy through suitably recondite means—she absolutely loathed *phoniness,* that pretentious public display of false feeling she associated with the high culture establishment. Two of the most significant poems in *Crystal Flowers* make this distinction perfectly clear, and, at the same time, together, are a perfect paradigm of the loves and hates of Camp sensibility. On the one hand, "I hate Beethoven": "Oh horrors!/ I hate Beethoven/ And I was brought up/ To revere him/ Adore him/ Oh horrors/ I hate Beethoven// I am hearing the/ 5th Symphony/ Led by Stokowsky/ It's being done heroically/ Cheerfully pompous/ Insistently infallible/ It says assertively/ Ja-Ja-Ja-Ja//Jawohl—Jawohl/ Pflicht—!—Pflicht!/ Jawohl!/ Herrliche!/ Pflicht!/ Deutsche Pflicht/ Ja-Ja-Ja-Ja/ And heads nod/ In the German way/ Devoutly—/affirmatively/ Oh—horrors."[17]

Pomposity, dutifulness, the heavy, automatic response to an implicitly patriarchal infallibility—such are the things which fill Florine Stettheimer with horror. What inspires her with delight is the very opposite of all that is heavy, dutiful, solemn, or imposed by authority; she articulates her loves in a hymn to lightness, lace, feminine sensibility, and the goddess of it, her mother; a paean to the adored textures, sounds and objets d'art of childhood: "And Things I loved—/ Mother in a low-cut dress/ Her neck like alabaster/ A laced up bodice of Veronese green/ A skirt all puffs of deeper shades/ With flounces of point lace/ Shawls of Blonde and Chantilly/ Fichues of Honeton and Point d'Esprit/ A silk jewel box painted with morning glories/ Filled with ropes of Roman pearls/ . . . Embroidered dresses of white Marseilles/ Adored sash of pale watered silk/ Ribbons with gay Roman stripes/ A carpet strewn with flower bouquets/ Sèvres vases and gilt console tables/ Mother reading us fairy tales/ When sick in bed with childhood ills—/ All loved and unforgettable thrills."[18] Mother, lace, and fairy tales belong to the cherished world of dream-artifice; Beethoven, German solemnity, and hollow affirmation to that of dreary falsehood: nowhere is she more forthright about the distinction.

With that distinction in mind, one might well raise some questions about conventional notions of an art of social concern itself,

especially as these have recently been articulated in our own country. Must a public art of this kind be solemn, pompous, and alien-
ated? Or can it, on the contrary, be personal, witty, and satirical?
Can one's friends and family be seen as participants in history, and,
conversely, can the major figures of history be envisioned as inti-
mates, as part of one's own experience? Is it possible for imagination
and reality to converge in a lively, problematic image of contemporary society? Must history, in other words, be conceived of as something idealized, distant, and dead that happened to other people, or
is it something that involves the self? And what, precisely, are the
boundaries between the public and the private? Why has such a
distinction been made in the creation of art? All these issues are
raised, although hardly resolved, by the art of Florine Stettheimer.

On the simplest level of historical awareness and political con-
viction, there is Florine Stettheimer's lifelong admiration for America and Americanness: her own kind of patriotism. Both *West Point*
of 1917, now at the U.S. Military Academy, and *New York* of 1918,
in the collection of Virgil Thomson, offer examples of it, warmed
by the glow of the expatriate recently reunited with her birthplace
—the Stettheimer sisters and their mother had returned to New
York from Europe at the outbreak of World War I. *West Point,*
commemorating a visit of August 29, 1917, is a pictorial record—a
topographically accurate continuous narrative—of the Stettheimers'
trip to the Military Academy by Hudson Dayliner, by car, and on
foot. The composition features the symbolic flag and eagle, and
places George Washington—a lifelong idol of Florine's and perhaps, as father of her country, an apotheosis of the missing Stettheimer *père*—at the heart of the composition in the form of a bronze
copy of the 1853 Union Square equestrian portrait by Henry Kirke
Brown (which had recently been obtained by Clarence P. Towne
and dedicated in 1915). In *New York,* Washington plays a relatively
minor role as a tiny statue in front of the Subtreasury, at the end
of a long vista, but the painting is really an homage to another
symbol of American grandeur: the Statue of Liberty. The painting,
inspired by Woodrow Wilson's visit to the Peace Conference of
1918, is minutely detailed, and the historic implications of the pano-
rama are underscored by the palpability of the statue, built up in

relief of putty impasto covered with gold leaf, so that, literally as well as figuratively, Liberty stands out.[19]

Although Stettheimer can hardly be counted among the ranks of notable activists in the cause of racial equality, it is nevertheless true that black people figured quite regularly in her work, from the time of *Jenny and Genevieve* of about 1915 to that of *Four Saints in Three Acts,* the Gertrude Stein–Virgil Thomson opera for which she designed the sets and costumes in 1934. Her sympathy for black causes can, in addition, be inferred not merely from her work but from her close friendship with one of the staunchest supporters of black culture, the music critic, belle lettrist, and bon vivant, Carl Van Vechten. One of the most ambitious and complex of all Florine Stettheimer's social investigations of the twenties is devoted to a black environment, the segregated beach of *Asbury Park South,* now in the collection of Fisk University. The subject, which also inspired a poem,[20] may well have been suggested by Van Vechten, whose portrait she did in 1922, and who figures in the reviewing stand to the left in *Asbury Park South.*[21] An extraordinarily active promoter of black cultural interests, Van Vechten spent most of his free hours in Harlem literary salons and nightclubs during the twenties. He loved and publicized jazz, which, he maintained in his capacity as a music critic in 1924, was "the only music of value produced in America." The black writer James Weldon Johnson said in the early days of the Negro literary and artistic renaissance that Carl Van Vechten, by means of his personal efforts and his articles in journals, did more than anyone else in the country to forward it. Walter White, founder of the NAACP, was a close friend, as were literary figures like Langston Hughes, Countee Cullen and Zora Neale Hurston. In his later avatar as a photographer, Van Vechten created an extensive gallery of portraits of blacks prominent in the arts; he received an honorary doctorate in 1955 from Fisk University, to which he donated his collection of black musical literature and where he established the Florine Stettheimer Collection of Books on the Fine Arts.

The extent of Van Vechten's involvement with black culture was noted in the pages of *Vanity Fair* in the form of a caricature of the music critic in blackface by his friend Covarrubias, the Mexican draftsman, and a popular song of about 1924, "Go Harlem," advised its listeners to "go inspectin' like Van Vechten." Van Vechten's parties were famous for their heady mixture of black and white celebrities; Bessie Smith might be found rubbing shoulders with Helena Rubinstein. Florine noted in the pages of her diary meeting Paul Robeson and Somerset Maugham at one of Carl and Fania's parties.[22] In 1926, Van Vechten published *Nigger Heaven*, a brilliant, poignant, unstereotyped, and sexy novel about various social circles in Harlem, in which the author reveals the richness and authenticity of black culture and, at the same time, the tragedy that might ensue for the more educated members of Harlem society when they tried to enter the white world.[23] Van Vechten dedicated this work to the Stettheimer sisters, and Florine thanked him for her copy with a poem: "Darling Moses// Your Black Chillun/ Are floundering/ In the sea// Gentle Moses// The waves don't part/ To let us Travel free// Holy Moses// Lead us on/ To Happyland/ We'll follow/ Thee// Dear Carlo, this is to you in admiration of your courage. Florine, West End, August 1st, 1926."[24]

The impact of Van Vechten's passion for all aspects of black cultural expression was felt not only by Florine but also by his friend Covarrubias, whose impressions of nightlife in Harlem appeared in *Vanity Fair* in the twenties and were published as *Negro Drawings* in 1927. Certainly, these drawings offer stylistic parallels to the figure style of *Asbury Park South* in their sinuous compression and simplication of form, which Parker Tyler, in the case of Stettheimer's painting, has likened to paleolithic art or Rhodesian rock painting.[25] We may feel that works such as Covarrubias's or Stettheimer's are demeaning or caricatural, but at the time, they were viewed by both blacks and whites as homages to black elegance, grace, and energy.[26] Florine's vision of blacks—campy, satirical, and admiring at once, idiosyncratic, clearly a vision of high life and high times rather than of a worthy but unjustly treated proletariat—is very different from the blander ideal of the benign melting pot, which informs the iconography of a work like Lucienne Bloch's mural *The Cycle of a Woman's Life* (see Figure 1 in Chapter 4), completed for the New York Women's House of Detention in 1936 under the New Deal. In some ways, Florine Stettheimer's vision is closer to today's sensibility in the way it stresses racial uniqueness and self-identification rather than brotherhood at the expense of authentic ethnicity. But here again, the issue of public versus private expression comes into question: Stettheimer's work is intended for a relatively restricted and, of course, voluntary audience. It does not preach or offer solace. The other is meant for a public place—a prison at that—and is therefore fated to uplift and to promulgate a consoling mythology.

But perhaps the most consistent and ambitious expressions of Stettheimer's social consciousness are the four *Cathedrals,* a series that engaged her intermittently from approximately 1929 until her death in 1944. All of them are in the Metropolitan Museum; all are large-scale—about 60 by 50 inches—and packed with incident. In these, her masterpieces, she ingeniously and inextricably mingles the realms of reality and fantasy, observation and invention. The *Cathedrals* are grand, secular shrines dedicated to the celebration of American life, as exemplified in its most cosmopolitan, expansive, yet for Stettheimer, most intimately known city: New York. She subdivides this celebration of urban excitements into four major categories: the world of theater and film in the case of *Cathedrals of Broadway,* ca. 1929; the world of shops and high society in *Cathedrals of Fifth Avenue,* ca. 1931; the world of money and politics in *Cathedrals of Wall Street,* ca. 1939; and finally, the world of art—her own particular world within New York—in the unfinished *Cathedrals of Art.* The compositions are centralized and hieratic, as befits secular icons presided over by contemporary cult figures, yet this centralization is never ponderous or static, but, on the contrary, airy and mobile, energized by fluid, swirling rhythms, animated by a weightless, breezy sort of dynamism. The iconography of the *Cathedrals* is both serious and lightheartedly outrageous, giving evidence of the artist's view that admiration and social criticism are far from mutually exclusive. The color is sparkling, the drawing soft and crackling at the same time. Each *Cathedral,* in addition to celebrating a permanent aspect of New York life, at the same time commemorates a particular event—in the case of *Cathedrals of Broadway,* for instance, the shift from silent films to talkies. In the center, golden Silence is roped off beneath a newsreel-gray image of Jimmy Walker opening the New York baseball season, while the blazing marquees of the Strand and the Roxy to left and right proclaim the advent of the talking film. *Cathedrals of Fifth Avenue,* besides celebrating a society wedding and the glories of Hudnut's, Tiffany's, B. Altman's, Maillard's, and Delmonico's, is also a commemoration of Lindbergh's flight—the hero can be seen parading in an open car in the background to the left. In all of the *Cathedrals,* Florine, her sisters, and her interesting friends figure prominently; they are part of New York's ongoing life, participants in historic occasions. In *Cathedrals of Fifth Avenue,* for instance, above the hood of the car decorated with a dollar sign on the right, appear the artist and her sisters; between the family group and the wedding party are Charles Demuth, with Mrs. Valentine Dudensing and her daughter in front of him and Muriel Draper leaning on Max Ewing to his left. Arnold Genthe is photographing the ceremony, and Mrs. Walter Rosen stands next to him in yellow.[27]

Florine's celebration of her city finds close parallels, once more, in her poetry. Not only do several poems explicitly deal with the varied joys of the city, but in one untitled work the very brand-name explicitness of that loving celebration is reiterated: "My attitude is one of Love/ is all adoration/ for all the fringes/ all the color/ all tinsel creation/ I like slippers gold/ I like oysters cold/ and my garden of mixed flowers/ and the sky full of towers/ and traffic in the streets/ and Maillard's sweets/ and Bendel's clothes/ and Nat Lewis hose/ and Tappé's window arrays/ and crystal fixtures/ and my pictures/ and Walt Disney cartoons/ and colored balloons."[28]

Yet the *Cathedrals* depend upon more than mere affection and a sense of personal participation for their striking unity of feeling and design. Their complex yet highly readable structure may, indeed, strike a familiar chord. Despite basic differences of attitude, there is a strange and, as it were, distilled reminiscence of the murals of Diego Rivera in these works. A comparison with the revolutionary murals of the Mexican artist may seem farfetched or even perverse; nevertheless, the Ministry of Education frescoes in Mexico City were published in this country in 1929,[29] the year of the earliest of the *Cathedral* paintings, and certain common features may be observed to exist in Rivera's *The Billionaires* or his *Song of the*

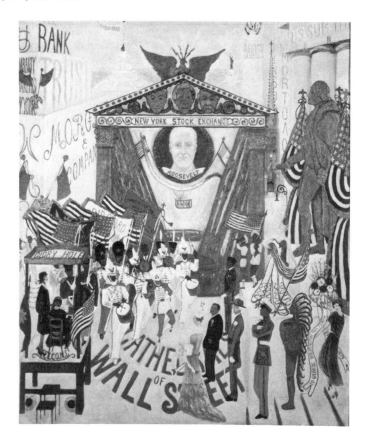

5. Florine Stettheimer. *Cathedrals of Wall Street*

Revolution and Stettheimer's *Cathedrals of Broadway* or *Cathedrals of Wall Street.* It might also be kept in mind that both Stettheimer and Rivera had made extensive art tours of Europe and had returned to their native lands thoroughly familiar with both traditional European artistic culture and the new pictorial experiments of the avant-garde. Both were highly responsive to the popular culture and folk art of their own nations. Both regarded their native lands with critical and loving eyes, and both felt free, for the purposes of their message—and because both folk and vanguard art encouraged it—to incorporate verbal elements into the pictorial fabric of their works, a procedure which Stettheimer plays to the hilt in *Cathedrals of Fifth Avenue,* where "Tiffany's" is spelled out in jewels, "Alt-man's" in household furnishings and dry goods.

The third of the series, *Cathedrals of Wall Street,* signed and dated 1939 but probably finished after that date, is worth studying in considerable detail, partly because a good deal of material relating to its genesis is available, partly because it unites in a single, scintil-lating image so many of Stettheimer's responses to the social issues of her time, as well as her political commitments—in her own terms, of course [5]. In *Wall Street* Big Business confronts popular pag-eantry; the historic past confronts contemporary American life; her beloved New York shelters the major representatives of her equally beloved New Deal. The painting then is a satiric icon—almost Byzantine in its symmetry, frontality, and golden effulgence—but an icon up-to-date and jazzy in its staccato rhythms and concrete detail; presiding over this icon are the Father, Son, and Holy Ghost of a patriotic Trinity: Washington, Roosevelt, and the American Eagle.

Cathedrals of Wall Street is an homage to Mrs. Roosevelt, elegant in an Eleanor-blue gown in the center of the piece. She is escorted by Mayor La Guardia, and is about to be thrilled by "The Star-Spangled Banner" intoned by Grace Moore, who stands to the right center. Among the other identified figures are Michael Ericson in an American Legion uniform; Michael J. Sullivan, a Civil War veteran; Claget Wilson; and an Indian chief.[30] Yet perhaps primar-ily, *Cathedrals of Wall Street* is dedicated to the memory of George Washington; the artist herself is depicted offering his statue a bou-quet inscribed "To George Washington from Florine St." at the far right. Stettheimer's affection for the father of her country was long-standing, going back at least as far as the outbreak of World War I. The sitting room in her Beaux-Arts apartment included a bust of Washington enshrined in a niche. The pages of her diary make reverent reference to painting the figure of Washington in *Cathe-drals of Wall Street* on the anniversary of his birth. She notes: "Feb. 22. *Washington's Day* 1939—I put lots of gold on Washington"; on Feb. 22, 1940: "Washington's day—Painted all day—Washington in the painting."

As far as the Roosevelts were concerned, her affections, though of more recent vintage, were not less fervent. Evidently, she wanted Van Vechten to introduce her to Mrs. Roosevelt because she so admired her, and of course, wished to put her into her painting, but Van Vechten evidently did not know the First Lady.[31] Florine was an ardent supporter of FDR. In her diary she notes: "Nov. Fifth 1940—Have just registered my vote for Roosevelt"; on the 6th: "I took off my tel. receiver at seven A.M.—'Roosevelt' said the voice instead of 'good morning' "; on Jan. 2, 1941: "Inauguration Day—Thank goodness it came off—heard oath and speech. . . ." On Oct. 24, 1940, she had noted with dismay: "McBride and Clagg [Claget Wilson] for Wilkie oh horrors! Showed them Cathedrals of Wall Street and Clagg in marine uniform in it."

The date inscribed on the painting suggests still further and even more concrete memorial connections. Nineteen-thirty-nine was the year dedicated to celebrating the 150th anniversary of George Washington's inauguration in New York. In *George Washington in New York,* a far less ambitious work which, done in the same year, may well be related to *Cathedrals of Wall Street,* Stettheimer makes her point by simply juxtaposing a bust of George with the New York skyline. The inauguration had taken place just where she set her Wall Street painting, on the steps of the old Subtreasury Building, then Federal Hall, at Wall and Nassau Streets, a site marked by John Quincy Adams Ward's 1883 bronze statue of Washington, so prominently featured in the painting. The major civic event of 1939, the New York World's Fair, like *Cathedrals of Wall Street,* was planned to commemorate this momentous occasion, and, like the painting, was intended as a tribute to the father of our country, as the cover of the special "World's Fair Supplement" to the *New York Times* magazine section clearly indicates.

The first diary notations about *Cathedrals of Wall Street* occur in 1938, when plans for various First Inaugural commemorations, and, of course, for the New York World's Fair, the biggest celebration of Washington's inauguration of all, were well under way. On April 18 of that year, Florine makes reference to putting Grace Moore singing "The Star-Spangled Banner" into *Wall Street,* and to meeting the celebrated singer at Rose Laird's beauty salon. On April 19, she notes: "Started to stain the outlines of my new painting 'Cathedrals of Wall Street.' " She was evidently still working on it well into 1940, when, according to notations in her diary, she went to visit the Stock Exchange and had her friend, the lawyer Joseph Solomon, bring her ticker tape to copy. The date 1939 inscribed on the painting, then, refers to the event it commemorates rather than the year the painting was actually completed.

All during the period preceding the inauguration celebrations, sources of inspiration for the artist's project offered themselves in the press. For example, although it is not specifically related to the Washington festivities themselves, a major illustrated article by Elliot V. Bell titled "What is Wall Street?" which ran in the *New York Times* of Jan. 2, 1938, almost sounds like a description of the subject and setting of Stettheimer's painting. The writer discusses the new focus of attention which has shifted to Wall Street in order to counteract the business depression, and includes what might be considered a verbal equivalent of major features of the canvas: "The geographical center of the district lies at the intersection where Broad Street ends and Nassau Street begins. Here on one corner stands the Stock Exchange, on another J. P. Morgan's and on a third the outmoded temple of the old United States Subtreasury upon which the statue of George Washington stands with lifted hand to mark the site where the first President on April 30, 1789, took the oath of office. . . ."[32] On April 30, 1938, the *New York Times* ran an illustrated account of "A Patriotic Ceremony in Wall Street," subtitled "A view of the exercises in front of the Subtreasury Building yesterday commemorating the inauguration of George Washington as the first President of the United States." The report went on to describe the representatives of many patriotic organizations, military and naval groups with their massed colors which had joined the previous day in commemorating the first inauguration, which had taken place 149 years ago; the accompanying photograph is remarkably similar to the right-hand portion of Stettheimer's painting.[33]

In April of the following year, 1939, the 150th anniversary of the occasion, an eight-day reenactment of Washington's celebrated trip from Mount Vernon to New York took place, with the participants decked out in eighteenth-century costume, traveling from Virginia to New York in a 160-year-old coach and crossing from New Jersey to Manhattan by barge. On April 30, Inauguration Day itself, there was a ceremony in front of Federal Hall during which wreaths like the ones in Stettheimer's painting were reverently laid at the feet of Washington's statue; all the patriotic societies paraded, and, according to the *New York Times* report, "the nearly empty financial district . . . echoed and reechoed the blaring music of military bands."[34] Denys Wortman, an artist and cartoonist who took the part of Washington, was received by Mayor La Guardia at City Hall.[35]

None of these celebrations could, however, match in elaborateness or scale the climactic event of the eight-day journey—the reenactment of the First Inaugural. The reconstructed ceremony took place beneath the colossal 68-foot-high statue of the Father of Our Country on Constitution Mall as part of the opening day festivities on April 30 of the New York World's Fair; Denys Wortman and his costumed entourage were whisked from Manhattan to Flushing Meadows by speedboat for the occasion.[36]

All these events must have struck an answering spark in the breast of someone who admired Washington as much as Florine Stettheimer did, and many of the reports and announcements of these happenings were illustrated with drawings and photographs which may well have added fuel to the fire. One can imagine Stettheimer's enthusiasm for a commemoration which united her favorite historic personage with her favorite contemporary entertainment —George Washington with the World's Fair. And she adored the Fair, visited it almost daily during the spring and summer of 1939, and, according to her sister Ettie, hoped to be asked to commemorate it in her art, a hope which remained unfulfilled. *Cathedrals of Wall Street* must then serve by proxy as her pictorial tribute to the exuberance and optimism—alas, ill founded—with which the Fair approached the future.

At the same time, *Cathedrals of Wall Street* hardly seems to call down unmixed blessings on the present-day Republic. George Washington seems a bit startled by the presence of Bernard Baruch,

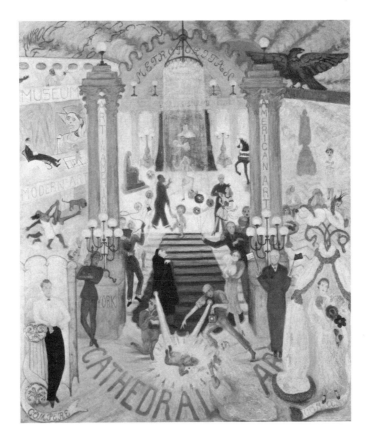

6. Florine Stettheimer. *Cathedrals of Art*

John D. Rockefeller, and J. P. Morgan in the pediment of the Stock Exchange. The ubiquity of gold seems to have more than Byzantine implications; it impinges on the very rays of light infiltrating the floor of the Exchange. And the juxtaposition of Salvation Army and Stock Exchange offers a trenchant pictorial paraphrase of George Bernard Shaw's pointed question from the end of *Major Barbara*: "What price salvation?" Washington is both the guardian of and admittedly a bit peripheral to the modern world of drum majorettes and high finance.

*   *   *

Stettheimer's final work in the *Cathedrals* series celebrated that aspect of New York achievement with which she was most intimately connected: the world of art. *Cathedrals of Art* [6], dated 1942 but left unfinished at the time of her death in 1944, is her ultimate pictorial statement about the inextricable connection between public and private, between the friends she cherished and the works of art to which they dedicated their lives. The grand, three-part setting, dominated by the red-carpeted main staircase of the old Metropolitan Museum, clearly distinguishes art *in* America, the province of the Museum of Modern Art (to the left), from *American* art, the realm of the Whitney Museum (to the right), with the Metropolitan Museum itself providing that overarching tradition which—spatially as well as chronologically—lies behind both. On the crossbar of the stretcher, in 1941, Florine identified the work as "Our Dawn of Art." And indeed, in the foreground, baby Art—based on a recently acquired statue of Eros, depicted here as born drawing— is being photographed by George Platt Lynes in a blaze of light, while being worshiped by a female art lover to his right.[37] Baby Art ascends the stairs, hand in hand with the Metropolitan's director, Francis Henry Taylor, to join curator of paintings Harry B. Wehle, standing at the top of the stairs with a young woman holding a clearly labeled "prize." The red-carpeted staircase is flanked by museum directors, critics, and art dealers; perhaps a certain reminiscence of Raphael's *School of Athens* gives added resonance to the composition. Among the art-world notables present are Alfred Stieglitz on the staircase to the left, grandly cloaked and turning his profile upward to follow youthful Art's progress; A. Everett (Chick) Austin, Jr., the enterprising director of the Wadsworth Atheneum, standing with folded arms at the base of the left-hand column inscribed "Art in America"; his counterpart at the base of the right-hand column, inscribed "American Art," is Stettheimer's friend and supporter, the critic Henry McBride, with "Stop" and "Go" signs in his hand.

In the center of the composition, Francis Henry Taylor leads the infant to the High Altar of the Cathedral of Art in the form of a portrait, perhaps reminiscent of Mrs. Stettheimer, by one of the artists whom Florine most admired, Frans Hals. This sedate and portly figure from the past is set in opposition to a sprightly and up-to-date young female figure, also directly on central axis, labeled "cocktail dress"—perhaps meant to represent the modern feminine ideal as opposed to the more traditional one.[38]

In the left-hand "panel" of what might well be considered a triptych, Art plays hopscotch on a Mondrian laid out at the feet of Alfred Barr, Jr., seated most appropriately in what looks like a Corbusier chair before two striking Picassos. Immediately beneath Barr, the two *Women on the Beach* break loose from their canvas in front of the Douanier Rousseau's lion. In the upper part of the right-hand "panel," dedicated to the Whitney Museum, stands Juliana Force in front of a sculptured figure by Gertrude Vanderbilt Whitney, guarded by an American eagle. To the lower right and lower left foreground, isolated by a screen and a white-and-gold lily-topped canopy respectively, stand Robert Locher (an old friend), and Stettheimer herself, as *compère* and *commère* of the spectacle—an idea, incidentally, that the artist probably derived from *Four Saints in Three Acts*. The two figure as patron saints or intercessors between the world of art and its audience. *Cathedrals of Art*, then, is not only a tribute to art but to New York's art institutions and to the people who run them. The only other painting about art that is as original in both its richness of allusion and its sense of intimate personal involvement is of course Courbet's *Painter's Studio*. Like Courbet's *Studio*, *Cathedrals of Art* is an *allégorie réelle*, an allegory that takes its terms from experienced reality, and as such, like Courbet's work, it emphasizes the role of friendship, of mutual support and of contemporary inventiveness in sustaining a living art.

In "Public Use of Art," an important article which appeared in *Art Front* in 1936, Meyer Schapiro inveighed against the public murals of the New Deal, seeing in "their seemingly neutral glorification of work, progress and national history the instruments of a class"—the dominating class of the nation. "The conceptions of such mural paintings," Schapiro maintained, "rooted in naïve, sentimental ideas of social reality, cannot help betray the utmost banality and poverty of invention."[39] While one may feel that Schapiro is too sweeping in his condemnation of the public art of his day, and that

Stettheimer's playful and in many ways arcane creations hardly offer a viable alternative to the mural programs sponsored under the New Deal, his criticism is nevertheless relevant to Stettheimer's art. Her ideas of social reality, if idiosyncratic, are neither naïve nor sentimental, her pictorial invention the opposite of "banal" or "poor." Nor is her vision, in *Cathedrals of Art,* totally affirmative.

Beneath the glowing admiration for American institutions and personae in this work, as in the other paintings of the *Cathedrals* series, exists a pointed and knowing critique of them as well. The *Cathedrals,* as I have indicated, are by no means pure affirmations of American, or even New York, values. The most effective revelations of social reality are not necessarily either intentional or from the left, as both Engels and Georg Lukács have reminded us. Balzac, upholder of monarchy, was in fact the most acute and critical analyst of the social reality of his time. Look again at *Wall Street;* or look again at *Cathedrals of Art,* with each little chieftain smugly ensconced in his or her domain, the dealers feverishly waving their artists' balloons or clutching their wares, the critic with his mechanical signals, the avid photographers—and the blinded, worshipful public.

Florine Stettheimer, the artist, existed in this world, it is true, but still somewhat apart from it—as her painting exists apart from the major currents of her time. She knew herself to be, as an artist, a peripheral if cherished figure, unappreciated and unbought by the broader public. She may indeed, in her discreet way, have felt rather bitter about this larger neglect. After a disastrous exhibition at Knoedler's in 1916, although she would often show a work or two at group shows at the Whitney, the Carnegie Institute, or the Society of Independent Artists, she never had a major retrospective until 1946, after her death.[40]

In a poem from *Crystal Flowers,* Stettheimer succinctly sums up the position of art in a capitalist society: "Art is spelled with a capital A/ And capital also backs it/ Ignorance also makes it sway/ The chief thing is to make it pay/ In a quite dizzy way/ Hurrah— Hurrah—."[41] Here, certainly, is social consciousness about art if ever there was.

Notes

1. The major sources of information about Florine Stettheimer are the exhibition catalogue *Florine Stettheimer*, New York, Museum of Modern Art, 1946, edited by Henry McBride; and Parker Tyler's *Florine Stettheimer: A Life in Art*, New York, 1963. In addition, the Florine Stettheimer archive in the Beinecke Rare Book and Manuscript Library of Yale University contains the manuscript (unfortunately mutilated by her sister Ettie's scissors) of Florine's diary, as well as typed and manuscript versions of her poetry. Recent publications include the exhibition catalogues *Florine Stettheimer: An Exhibition of Paintings, Watercolors, Drawings*, Low Memorial Library, Columbia University, 1973; *Florine Stettheimer: Still Lifes, Portraits and Pageants 1910 to 1942*, Institute of Contemporary Art, Boston, 1980; and an article by Barbara Zucker, "Autobiography of Visual Poems," *Art News*, Feb. 1977, pp. 68–73.

2. *Philosophy [An Autobiographical Fragment]* was originally published in 1917; *Love Days* in 1923. Both were republished along with a group of short stories and an English translation of her doctoral dissertation, written in 1907 for Freiburg University, on William James's *The Will to Believe* in *Memorial Volume of and by Ettie Stettheimer*, New York, 1951.

3. Stettheimer also painted an individual *Portrait of My Mother* (1925), her best work in the opinion of Henry McBride (Museum of Modern Art catalogue, 1946, p. 39).

4. For a somewhat different interpretation of the significance of the bouquet, see Tyler, p. 15.

5. Florine Stettheimer, *Crystal Flowers*, New York, 1949. This edition of Florine's verses was published after her death by her sister, Ettie, who also provided an introduction.

6. All references to the diary refer to the manuscript in the Beinecke Rare Book and Manuscript Library mentioned in n. 1 above. Her comments range from remarks on the Aegina Pediment in Munich; to her ideas and feelings about the old masters viewed on visits to Italian churches, museums, and palaces in 1906; to comments on a Rodin Exhibition in 1910 and on some Stücks seen at the Munich Secession. In 1912, she notes, on a trip to Madrid, that "the beauty of the Titian Venus and the Danae" is "intoxicatingly beautiful" and that *Las Meninas*, to her surprise, "had the quality of realism attributed to it by those who write about it." In Toledo, she admits that she doesn't think El Greco so marvelous. In Paris she exclaims: "I can't bear Carpeaux. His Hugolin [sic] is stupid . . ." and declares Regnault's *Salome*, now in the Metropolitan Museum, "an abomination." She admires Manet and declares Monet's "new Venice painting the most attractive things he has done so far." Her reaction to Gustave Moreau's work is measured. In 1913, she notes a very good loan show of van Gogh flowers.

7. Miss Fish was an extremely popular cartoonist for the cognoscenti who read *Vanity Fair*. A full-page advertisement for her *High Society: A Book of Satirical Drawings*, by Fish, which appeared in *Vanity Fair*, Nov. 1920, p. 24, claimed that " 'High Society' is the smartest book of the season" and that ". . . the patterns of the flappers' frocks are like laces and hangings by Beardsley." There has been an exhibition of Miss Fish's work in New York recently, but I have been unable to locate a reference to it.

8. E. Stettheimer, *Crystal Flowers*, introduction, p. iii.

9. Manuscript version, Beinecke Library, dated about 1917.

10. For a fuller discussion of *Beauty Contest*, see the exhibition catalogue *Women Artists: 1550–1950*, by A. S. Harris and L. Nochlin, Los Angeles County Museum of Art, 1976, p. 267.

11. Susan Sontag, "Notes on 'Camp' " (1964), in *Against Interpretation and Other Essays*, New York, 1967, p. 277.

12. Sontag, p. 287.

13. Sontag, p. 277. For a more recent and equally provocative discussion of Camp and associated issues, see Brigid Brophy's *Prancing Novelist: A Defense of Fiction in the Form of a Critical Biography in Praise of Ronald Firbank*, New York, 1973, especially pp. 171–73; but also 406–7 for the social subversiveness of Wilde's and Firbank's fictions, their emancipation of women and proletarians; and pp. 551–59 for *Prancing Nigger*.

14. *Crystal Flowers*, p. 78. Florine did not intend her poems for publication. This assumption of privacy may have something to do with their remarkable frankness.

15. *Crystal Flowers*, p. 43.

16. *Crystal Flowers*, p. 42.

17. This version of the poem and its punctuation are taken from the manuscript in the Beinecke Library, IV–VI.

18. Manuscript, Beinecke Library, VII–IX.

19. For a poem related to this painting beginning: "Then back to New York . . . ," see *Crystal Flowers*, p. 79.

20. Manuscript, Beinecke, IV–VI. "Asbury Park" begins: "It swings/it rings/it's full of noisy things. . . ."

21. Other friends present are: Van Vechten's wife, the actress Fania Marinoff; Marcel Duchamp; Avery Hopwood; Paul Thenevaz.

22. Most of the information about Van Vechten is obtained from Bruce Kellner's excellent study, *Carl Van Vechten and the Irreverent Decades*, Norman, Oklahoma, 1968. For a different, far more critical view of Van Vechten's relationship to Harlem and black culture, see Nathan Irvin Higgins, *Harlem Renaissance*, Oxford and New York, 1971, pp. 93–118. Not surprisingly, Van Vechten was not only an aficionado of black culture, but also the major promoter of Ronald Firbank in this country (Higgins, p. 95). It was Van Vechten who convinced Firbank to change the title of his *Sorrow in Sunlight* to *Prancing Nigger* when it was published in this country (Higgins, p. 112).

23. See Kellner, p. 202.

24. Manuscript, Beinecke, VII–IX. Evidently Carl Van Vechten typed up copies of Florine's letters to him—those about his books—and sent them, after Florine's death, to her sister Ettie.

25. Tyler, p. 131.

26. See, for instance, the introduction to Miguel Covarrubias, *Negro Drawings*, New York, 1927, by Frank Crowninshield, in which it is claimed that Covarrubias is "the first important artist in America . . . to bestow upon our Negro anything like the reverent attention . . . which Gauguin bestowed upon the natives of the South Seas" (np).

27. These identifications appear in the Stettheimer Archives in the Metropolitan Museum. They seem to follow those established by Henry McBride, Museum of Modern Art catalogue, 1946, table of contents.

28. *Crystal Flowers*, p. 23.

29. See *The Frescoes of Diego Rivera*, introduction by E. Evans, New York, 1929.

30. Identifications from McBride, Museum of Modern Art catalogue, 1946, p. 48, and Stettheimer Archives, Metropolitan Museum. I have been unable to discover any account, in either newspapers or biographies of the First Lady, of a visit by Mrs. Roosevelt to Wall Street at the time the painting was begun. Perhaps further investigation will reveal such a visitation; until then, one might best consider it an invention of Stettheimer's.

31. Tyler, p. 107.

32. *New York Times Magazine*, Jan. 2, 1938. The piece begins with a consideration of government credit expansion, "tried to the tune of $20,000,000,000." Could this figure be a clue to the meaning of the "19,000,000,000" inscribed to the left and to the right of Roosevelt's head in the painting? It is close, if not exact. The article continues with a description of the ". . . blackened spires of Trinity Church" as opposed to the "sun lit docks of the East River . . ." and refers to the ". . . itinerant preachers [who] often take their stand outside the Bankers' Trust at the corner of Wall and Nassau Streets, exhorting the noon-time crowds of clerks and office boys to forsake Mammon and return to God . . ." in roughly the same spot that Stettheimer placed her Salvation Army "Glory Hole."

33. *New York Times*, April 30, 1938, p. 3.

34. *New York Times*, May 1, 1939, p. 8.

35. See such articles as "Reenactment . . . ," *New York Times*, Tues., April 25, 1939, p. 3, and "In Washington's Footsteps," by H. I. Broch, *New York Times Magazine*, Sun., April 30, 1939, p. 6, as well as accounts in *New York Times*, Mon., May 1, 1939, p. 8.

36. *New York Times*, May 1, 1939, p. 8, with photograph of ceremony.

37. Once more, the identifications are from McBride, Museum of Modern Art catalogue, 1946, p. 53, and the Metropolitan Museum Archives. For a lengthier discussion, see Tyler, pp. 74–78.

38. I have not been able to pin down any specific incident which may be said to have "inspired" *Cathedrals of Art*. There are, however, several possibilities which may have contributed to its genesis: for example, the recent appointment of Francis Henry Taylor as director on Jan. 8, 1940; the reinstallation of the paintings in almost all the galleries, a project nearing completion in Aug. 1941 (*Bulletin of the Metropolitan Museum*, Aug. 1941, pp. 163–165); or a contemporary costume show, held in the museum shortly before the artist began her painting, which featured a "cocktail dress" like the one that figures so prominently in her work (Tyler, p. 74).

39. Meyer Schapiro, "Public Use of Art," *Art Front*, Nov. 1936, p. 6. I am grateful to Dr. Greta Berman for calling this article to my attention.

40. A third exhibition, "The Flowers of Florine Stettheimer," organized by Kirk Askew Jr., was held at Durlacher Bros. in 1948.

41. *Crystal Flowers*, p. 26.

6

Eroticism and Female Imagery in Nineteenth-Century Art

Considering how much of Western art deals with themes that are overtly or covertly erotic, it is surprising how little serious attention has been paid to the specifically erotic implications of art works by scholars and critics.[1] While the psychosexual development of artists has been thoroughly investigated, mainly by psychiatrists, since the time of Freud, no similar interest has been shown in the erotic content of their works, unless, as is the case with certain Surrealist examples, it is simply too obvious to ignore. Even in the latter case, the approach to the erotic is generally descriptive and psychological rather than analytic and directed toward investigation of the socially determined concomitants and conventions of erotic imagery in different art groups during different periods.

It would seem that the world of erotic imagery is no more controlled by mere personal fantasy *in vacuo* than any other type of imagery in art. It is precisely in the nineteenth century—at a time when older prototypes and motifs were transformed by new needs and motivations—that the social basis of sexual myth stands out in clearest relief from the apparently "personal" erotic imagery of individual artists.

Certain conventions of eroticism are so deeply ingrained that one scarcely bothers to think of them: one is that the very term "erotic art" is understood to imply the specification "erotic-for-men." The very title of this investigation—"Eroticism and Female Imagery"—is actually redundant. There really *is* no erotic art in the nineteenth century which does *not* involve the image of women, and precious little before or after. The notion that erotic imagery is created out of male needs and desires even encompasses the relatively minor category of art created for or by homosexuals; it has always been *male* homosexuals who are taken into consideration, from Antiquity through Andy Warhol. Even in the case of art with lesbian themes, men were considered to be the audience: Courbet painted his scandalous *Sleep* [1] not for a *femme damnée* of the time, but rather for the former Turkish ambassador, Khalil Bey, who no doubt felt as invigorated by the spectacle of two voluptuous female nudes locked in each other's arms as he had by the delectably realistic *bas ventre* Courbet had previously executed to his specifications.

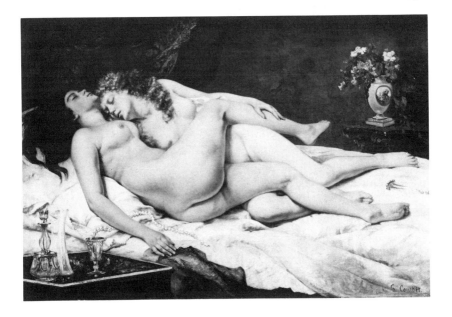

1. Gustave Courbet. *Sleep*

As far as one knows, there simply exists no art, and certainly no high art, in the nineteenth century based upon women's erotic needs, wishes, or fantasies. Whether the erotic object be breast or buttocks, shoes or corsets, a matter of pose or of prototype, the imagery of sexual delight or provocation has always been created *about* women for men's enjoyment, by men. This is, of course, not the result of some calculated plot on the part of men, but merely a reflection in the realm of art of woman's lack of her own erotic territory on the map of nineteenth-century reality. Man is not only the subject of all

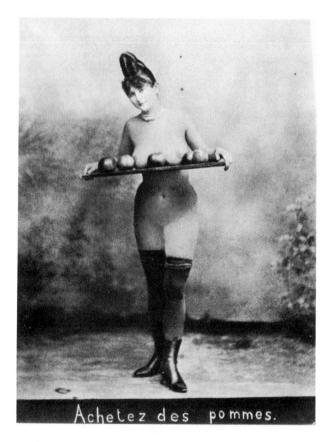

2. *Achetez des Pommes.* Anonymous nineteenth-century photograph

erotic predicates, but the customer for all erotic products as well, and the customer is always right. Controlling both sex and art, he and his fantasies conditioned the world of erotic imagination as well. Thus there seems to be no conceivable outlet for the expression of women's viewpoint in nineteenth-century art, even in the realm of pure fantasy.

This lack of a women's viewpoint in erotica is not merely a corollary of the fact that nineteenth-century art "mirrored" reality. It is obvious that there could have been no equivalent of Degas's or Lautrec's realistic and objective brothel scenes[2] painted by women and populated by men, given the nonexistence of such accommodations for feminine sexual needs. Women were never even permitted to *dream* about such things, much less bring them to life on canvas. Equally unthinkable would be such an egregiously unrealistic erotopia as *Turkish Bath*, populated by sloe-eyed, close-pressed, languid youths, and painted by an octogenarian Mme Ingres. Those who have no country have no language. Women have no imagery available—no accepted public language to hand—with which to express their particular viewpoint. And of course, one of the major elements involved in any successful language system is that it can be universally understood, so that its tropes have a certain mobility and elasticity, as it were—they can rise from the lowest levels of popular parlance to the highest peaks of great art.

While certainly low on the scale of artistic merit, a nineteenth-century photograph like *Achetez des Pommes* [2] nevertheless embodies one of the prime topoi of erotic imagery: comparison of the desirable body with ripe fruit, or more specifically, the likening of a woman's breasts to apples. *Achetez des Pommes* represents this image on the lowest level, to be sure, but the fruit or flower-breast metaphor can move easily up into higher esthetic realms: in Gauguin's *Tahitian Women with Mango Blossoms*, 1899 [3], the breasts of the women are obviously likened to both fruit and flower. As Wayne Andersen points out: "Gauguin used this image in Tahiti because the charm of it fitted in with his surroundings, and with his favorite myths about the Promised Land. In *Tahitian Women with Flowers*, a noble-featured Tahitian girl holds a tray of flowers beneath her bosom; the lushness of the presentation causes the breasts

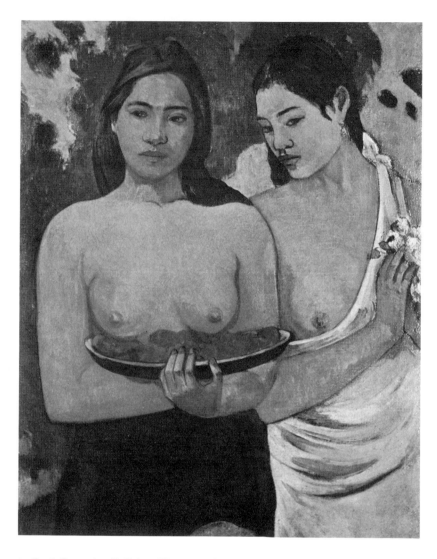

3. Paul Gauguin. *Tahitian Women with Mango Blossoms*

to appear as cornucopias from which all good things flow. . . ."[3]

In the case of Cézanne, Meyer Schapiro has devoted an entire article, "The Apples of Cézanne,"[4] to a convincing demonstration of the centrality of what one might call the apple-female sexuality syndrome in the artist's oeuvre. Professor Schapiro places the breast-apple metaphor in the context both of Western cultural history and of Cézanne's psychological development. There is obviously a time-honored connection, dignified by the sanction of high culture, between fruit and women's inviting nudity: apples and breasts have been associated from the time of Theocritus' pastoral verse down to Zola's eroticized paean to fruit in *Le Ventre de Paris*. Cézanne's *Amorous Shepherd* is convincingly interpreted in the light of this time-honored association by Professor Schapiro. Thus, despite the laughable triviality of *Achetez des Pommes* and its ilk as images, the echoes of a grand, universal, and time-honored metaphor still reverberate in them. In any case, man's erotic association of inviting fruit and a succulent, inviting area of the female body lends itself easily to artistic elevation: sanctioned by tradition and prototype, it may be raised to the level of the archetypal though it may indeed also sink to the level of the ridiculous.

No similar sanctions exist for the association of fruit with male sexuality, exemplified in a modern counterpart of *Achetez des Pommes* titled *Achetez des Bananes*. [4][5] While there may indeed be a rich underground feminine lore linking food—specifically bananas—with the male organ, such imagery remains firmly in the realm of private discourse, embodied in smirks and titters rather than works of art. Even today, the food-penis metaphor has no upward mobility, so to speak. While Sylvia Plath may compare—disappointedly—the male organ to turkey giblets, and Dr. William Rubin may describe—disapprovingly—the penis of the impotent male as "limp as a noodle," or to return to the banana metaphor, Philip Roth may nickname the heroine of *Portnoy's Complaint* "The Monkey," the linking of the male organ to food is always a figure of meiosis—an image of scorn, belittlement, or derision: it lowers and denigrates rather than elevates and universalizes the subject of the metaphor.

In the nineteenth century, and still today, the very idea—much less an available public imagery—of the male body as a source of

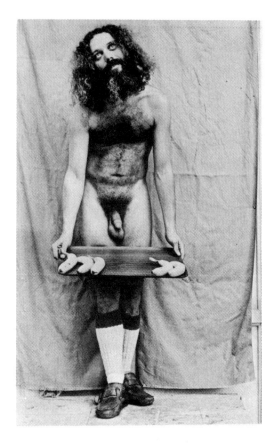

4. *Achetez des Bananes.* Photograph,
Linda Nochlin

gentle, inviting satisfaction for women's erotic needs, demands, and
daydreams is almost unheard of, and again not because of some
"male-chauvinist" plot in the arts, but because of the total situation
existing between men and women in society as a whole. The male
image is one of power, possession, and domination, the female one
of submission, passivity, and availability. The very language of love-
making attests to this, as does the erotic imagery of the visual arts.
Indeed, as John Berger has astutely pointed out, the female nude of
tradition can hardly call her sexuality her own. Says Berger: "I am

in front of a typical European nude. She is painted with extreme sensuous emphasis. Yet her sexuality is only superficially manifest in her actions or her own expression; in a comparable figure within other art traditions this would not be so. Why? Because for Europe, ownership is primary. The painting's sexuality is manifest not in what it shows but in the owner-spectator's (mine in this case) right to see her naked. Her nakedness is not a function of her sexuality but of the sexuality of those who have access to the picture. In the majority of European nudes there is a close parallel with the passivity which is endemic to prostitution."[6] One might add that the passivity implicit to the imagery of the naked woman in Western art is a function not merely of the attitude of the owner-spectator, but that of the artist-creator himself: indeed the myth of Pygmalion, revived in the nineteenth century, admirably embodies the notion of the artist as sexually dominant creator: man—the artist—fashioning from inert matter an ideal erotic object for himself, a woman cut to the very pattern of his desires.

There are, happily, signs of change which go beyond such ephemera as the male nude foldout popular in a magazine a few months ago. Years ago, Alice Neel, in her spectacular nude portrait of Joe Gould, took a step in the right direction. Sylvia Sleigh wittily reversed the conventional artist and model motif in her recent *Philip Golub Reclining*, representing a heavy-lidded male odalisque, recumbent against the foil of her own alert verticality. Miriam Schapiro furnished the miniature artist's studio in *Womanhouse* (in Los Angeles, winter-spring 1972) not only with a nude male model, but a still-life of bananas as well.

The growing power of woman in the politics of both sex and art is bound to revolutionize the realm of erotic representation. With the advent of more women directors, the film will have to reshape its current erotic clichés into more viable, less one-sided sexual imagery. All this still remains largely in the future. To borrow a phrase from Erica Jong's *Fruits and Vegetables*, a collection of poems which itself is a sign of the times in the freshness of its fruit imagery, "The poem about bananas has not yet been written."[7]

Notes

1. Two noteworthy exceptions in the recent literature immediately spring to mind: *Studies in Erotic Art,* sponsored by the Institute for Sex Research of Indiana University, edited by Theodore Bowie and Cornelia V. Christenson, containing articles by Bowie himself, Otto J. Brendel, Paul H. Gebbard, Robert Rosenblum, and Leo Steinberg; and Donald Posner's illuminating and convincing "Caravaggio's Homo-Erotic Early Works" which appeared in the Autumn 1971 *Art Quarterly.*

2. One can of course question to what extent such highly charged subjects could ever be considered "realistic" or "objective" in the nineteenth century, or at any time for that matter.

3. Wayne Andersen, *Gauguin's Paradise Lost,* New York, 1971, p. 247.

4. Meyer Schapiro, "The Apples of Cézanne," *The Avant-Garde* (*Art News Annual* XXXIV), New York, 1968, pp. 34–53.

5. Created by the author with the sympathetic cooperation of the male model at Vassar College.

6. John Berger, "The Past Seen from a Possible Future," *Selected Essays and Articles,* Penguin, 1972, p. 215.

7. Erica Jong, *Fruits and Vegetables,* New York, 1968, p. 13. The poem continues: "Southerners worry a lot about bananas. Their skin. And nearly everyone worries about the size of bananas, as if that had anything to do with flavor. Small bananas are sometimes quite sweet. But bananas are like poets: they only want to be told how great they are. Green bananas want to be told they're ripe. According to Freud, girls envy bananas. In America chocolate syrup and whipped cream have been known to enhance the flavor of bananas. This is called a *banana split.*"

7

Why Have There Been No Great Women Artists?

While the recent upsurge of feminist activity in this country has indeed been a liberating one, its force has been chiefly emotional—personal, psychological, and subjective—centered, like the other radical movements to which it is related, on the present and its immediate needs, rather than on historical analysis of the basic intellectual issues which the feminist attack on the status quo automatically raises.[1] Like any revolution, however, the feminist one ultimately must come to grips with the intellectual and ideological basis of the various intellectual or scholarly disciplines—history, philosophy, sociology, psychology, etc.—in the same way that it questions the ideologies of present social institutions. If, as John Stuart Mill suggested, we tend to accept whatever *is* as natural, this is just as true in the realm of academic investigation as it is in our social arrangements. In the former, too, "natural" assumptions must be questioned and the mythic basis of much so-called fact brought to light. And it is here that the very position of woman as an acknowledged outsider, the maverick "she" instead of the presumably neutral "one"—in reality the white-male-position-accepted-as-natural, or the hidden "he" as the subject of all scholarly predicates—is a decided advantage, rather than merely a hindrance or a subjective distortion.

In the field of art history, the white Western male viewpoint, unconsciously accepted as *the* viewpoint of the art historian, may—and does—prove to be inadequate not merely on moral and ethical grounds, or because it is elitist, but on purely intellectual ones. In revealing the failure of much academic art history, and a great deal of history in general, to take account of the unacknowledged value system, the very *presence* of an intruding subject in historical investigation, the feminist critique at the same time lays bare its conceptual smugness, its meta-historical naïveté. At a moment when all disciplines are becoming more self-conscious, more aware of the nature of their presuppositions as exhibited in the very languages and structures of the various fields of scholarship, such uncritical acceptance of "what is" as "natural" may be intellectually fatal. Just as Mill saw male domination as one of a long series of social injustices that had to be overcome if a truly just social order were to be created, so we may see the unstated domination of white male subjectivity as one in a series of intellectual distortions which must be corrected in order to achieve a more adequate and accurate view of historical situations.

It is the engaged feminist intellect (like John Stuart Mill's) that can pierce through the cultural-ideological limitations of the time and its specific "professionalism" to reveal biases and inadequacies not merely in dealing with the question of women, but in the very way of formulating the crucial questions of the discipline as a whole. Thus, the so-called woman question, far from being a minor, peripheral, and laughably provincial sub-issue grafted on to a serious, established discipline, can become a catalyst, an intellectual instrument, probing basic and "natural" assumptions, providing a paradigm for other kinds of internal questioning, and in turn providing links with paradigms established by radical approaches in other fields. Even a simple question like "Why have there been no great women artists?" can, if answered adequately, create a sort of chain reaction, expanding not merely to encompass the accepted assumptions of the single field, but outward to embrace history and the social sciences, or even psychology and literature, and thereby, from the outset, can challenge the assumption that the traditional divisions of intellectual inquiry are still adequate to deal with the meaningful questions of our time, rather than the merely convenient or self-generated ones.

Let us, for example, examine the implications of that perennial question (one can, of course, substitute almost any field of human endeavor, with appropriate changes in phrasing): "Well, if women really *are* equal to men, why have there never been any great women artists (or composers, or mathematicians, or philosophers, or so few of the same)?"

"Why have there been no great women artists?" The question tolls reproachfully in the background of most discussions of the so-called woman problem. But like so many other so-called questions involved in the feminist "controversy," it falsifies the nature of the issue at the same time that it insidiously supplies its own answer: "There are no great women artists because women are incapable of greatness."

The assumptions behind such a question are varied in range and sophistication, running anywhere from "scientifically proven" demonstrations of the inability of human beings with wombs rather than penises to create anything significant, to relatively open-minded wonderment that women, despite so many years of near-equality—and after all, a lot of men have had their disadvantages too —have still not achieved anything of exceptional significance in the visual arts.

The feminist's first reaction is to swallow the bait, hook, line and sinker, and to attempt to answer the question as it is put: that is, to dig up examples of worthy or insufficiently appreciated women artists throughout history; to rehabilitate rather modest, if interesting and productive careers; to "rediscover" forgotten flower painters or David followers and make out a case for them; to demonstrate that Berthe Morisot was really less dependent upon Manet than one had been led to think—in other words, to engage in the normal activity of the specialist scholar who makes a case for the importance of his very own neglected or minor master. Such attempts, whether undertaken from a feminist point of view, like the ambitious article on women artists which appeared in the 1858 *Westminster Review*,[2] or more recent scholarly studies on such artists as Angelica Kauffmann and Artemisia Gentileschi,[3] are certainly worth the effort, both in adding to our knowledge of women's achievement and of art history generally. But they do nothing to question the assumptions lying behind the question "Why have there been no great women artists?" On the contrary, by attempting to answer it, they tacitly reinforce its negative implications.

Another attempt to answer the question involves shifting the ground slightly and asserting, as some contemporary feminists do, that there is a different kind of "greatness" for women's art than for men's, thereby postulating the existence of a distinctive and recognizable feminine style, different both in its formal and its expressive qualities and based on the special character of women's situation and experience.

This, on the surface of it, seems reasonable enough: in general, women's experience and situation in society, and hence as artists, is different from men's, and certainly the art produced by a group of consciously united and purposefully articulate women intent on bodying forth a group consciousness of feminine experience might indeed be stylistically identifiable as feminist, if not feminine, art. Unfortunately, though this remains within the realm of possibility it has so far not occurred. While the members of the Danube School, the followers of Caravaggio, the painters gathered around Gauguin at Pont-Aven, the Blue Rider, or the Cubists may be recognized by certain clearly defined stylistic or expressive qualities, no such common qualities of "femininity" would seem to link the styles of women artists generally, any more than such qualities can be said to link women writers, a case brilliantly argued, against the most devastating, and mutually contradictory, masculine critical clichés, by Mary Ellmann in her *Thinking about Women.* [4] No subtle essence of femininity would seem to link the work of Artemesia Gentileschi, Mme Vigée-Lebrun, Angelica Kauffmann, Rosa Bonheur, Berthe Morisot, Suzanne Valadon, Käthe Kollwitz, Barbara Hepworth, Georgia O'Keeffe, Sophie Taeuber-Arp, Helen Frankenthaler, Bridget Riley, Lee Bontecou, or Louise Nevelson, any more than that of Sappho, Marie de France, Jane Austen, Emily Brontë, George Sand, George Eliot, Virginia Woolf, Gertrude Stein, Anaïs Nin, Emily Dickinson, Sylvia Plath, and Susan Sontag. In every instance, women artists and writers would seem to be closer to other artists and writers of their own period and outlook than they are to each other.

Women artists are more inward-looking, more delicate and nuanced in their treatment of their medium, it may be asserted. But which of the women artists cited above is more inward-turning than Redon, more subtle and nuanced in the handling of pigment than Corot? Is Fragonard more or less feminine than Mme Vigée-Lebrun? Or is it not more a question of the whole Rococo style of eighteenth-century France being "feminine," if judged in terms of a binary scale of "masculinity" versus "femininity"? Certainly, if daintiness, delicacy, and preciousness are to be counted as earmarks of a feminine style, there is nothing fragile about Rosa Bonheur's *Horse Fair*, nor dainty and introverted about Helen Frankenthaler's giant canvases. If women have turned to scenes of domestic life, or of children, so did Jan Steen, Chardin, and the Impressionists—Renoir and Monet as well as Morisot and Cassatt. In any case, the mere choice of a certain realm of subject matter, or the restriction to certain subjects, is not to be equated with a style, much less with some sort of quintessentially feminine style.

The problem lies not so much with some feminists' concept of what femininity is, but rather with their misconception—shared with the public at large—of what art is: with the naïve idea that art is the direct, personal expression of individual emotional experience, a translation of personal life into visual terms. Art is almost never that, great art never is. The making of art involves a self-consistent language of form, more or less dependent upon, or free from, given temporally defined conventions, schemata, or systems of notation, which have to be learned or worked out, either through teaching, apprenticeship, or a long period of individual experimentation. The language of art is, more materially, embodied in paint and line on canvas or paper, in stone or clay or plastic or metal—it is neither a sob story nor a confidential whisper.

The fact of the matter is that there have been no supremely great women artists, as far as we know, although there have been many interesting and very good ones who remain insufficiently investigated or appreciated; nor have there been any great Lithuanian jazz pianists, nor Eskimo tennis players, no matter how much we might wish there had been. That this should be the case is regrettable, but no amount of manipulating the historical or critical evidence will alter the situation; nor will accusations of male-chauvinist distortion of history. There *are* no women equivalents for Michelangelo or Rembrandt, Delacroix or Cézanne, Picasso or Matisse, or even, in very recent times, for de Kooning or Warhol, any more than there are black American equivalents for the same. If there actually were large numbers of "hidden" great women artists, or if there really should be different standards for women's art as opposed to men's —and one can't have it both ways—then what are feminists fighting for? If women have in fact achieved the same status as men in the arts, then the status quo is fine as it is.

But in actuality, as we all know, things as they are and as they have been, in the arts as in a hundred other areas, are stultifying, oppressive, and discouraging to all those, women among them, who did not have the good fortune to be born white, preferably middle class and, above all, male. The fault lies not in our stars, our hormones, our menstrual cycles, or our empty internal spaces, but in our institutions and our education—education understood to include everything that happens to us from the moment we enter this world of meaningful symbols, signs, and signals. The miracle is, in fact, that given the overwhelming odds against women, or blacks, that so many of both have managed to achieve so much sheer excellence, in those bailiwicks of white masculine prerogative like science, politics, or the arts.

It is when one really starts thinking about the implications of "Why have there been no great women artists?" that one begins to realize to what extent our consciousness of how things are in the world has been conditioned—and often falsified—by the way the most important questions are posed. We tend to take it for granted that there really is an East Asian Problem, a Poverty Problem, a Black Problem—and a Woman Problem. But first we must ask ourselves who is formulating these "questions," and then, what purposes such formulations may serve. (We may, of course, refresh our memories with the connotations of the Nazis' "Jewish Problem.") Indeed, in our time of instant communication, "problems" are rapidly formulated to rationalize the bad conscience of those with power: thus the problem posed by Americans in Vietnam and Cambodia is referred to by Americans as the "East Asian Problem," whereas East Asians may view it, more realistically, as the "American Problem"; the so-called Poverty Problem might more directly be viewed as the "Wealth Problem" by denizens of urban ghettos or rural wastelands; the same irony twists the White Problem into its opposite, a Black Problem; and the same inverse logic turns up in the formulation of our own present state of affairs as the "Woman Problem."

Now the "Woman Problem," like all human problems, so-called (and the very idea of calling anything to do with human beings a "problem" is, of course, a fairly recent one) is not amenable to "solution" at all, since what human problems involve is reinterpretation of the nature of the situation, or a radical alteration of stance or program *on the part of the "problems" themselves.* Thus women and their situation in the arts, as in other realms of endeavor, are not a "problem" to be viewed through the eyes of the dominant male power elite. Instead, *women* must conceive of themselves as potentially, if not actually, equal subjects, and must be willing to look the facts of their situation full in the face, without self-pity, or cop-outs; at the same time they must view their situation with that high degree of emotional and intellectual commitment necessary to create a world in which equal achievement will be not only made possible but actively encouraged by social institutions.

It is certainly not realistic to hope that a majority of men, in the arts or in any other field, will soon see the light and find that it is in their own self-interest to grant complete equality to women, as some feminists optimistically assert, or to maintain that men themselves will soon realize that they are diminished by denying themselves access to traditionally "feminine" realms and emotional reactions. After all, there are few areas that are really "denied" to men, if the level of operations demanded be transcendent, responsible, or rewarding enough: men who have a need for "feminine" involvement with babies or children gain status as pediatricians or child psychologists, with a nurse (female) to do the more routine work; those who feel the urge for kitchen creativity may gain fame as master chefs; and, of course, men who yearn to fulfill themselves through what are often termed "feminine" artistic interests can find themselves as painters or sculptors, rather than as volunteer museum aides or part-time ceramists, as their female counterparts so often end up doing; as far as scholarship is concerned, how many men would be willing to change their jobs as teachers and researchers for those of unpaid, part-time research assistants and typists as well as full-time nannies and domestic workers?

Those who have privileges inevitably hold on to them, and hold tight, no matter how marginal the advantage involved, until compelled to bow to superior power of one sort or another.

Thus the question of women's equality—in art as in any other realm—devolves not upon the relative benevolence or ill-will of individual men, nor the self-confidence or abjectness of individual women, but rather on the very nature of our institutional structures themselves and the view of reality which they impose on the human beings who are part of them. As John Stuart Mill pointed out more than a century ago: "Everything which is usual appears natural. The subjection of women to men being a universal custom, any departure from it quite naturally appears unnatural."[5] Most men, despite lip service to equality, are reluctant to give up this "natural" order of things in which their advantages are so great; for women, the case is further complicated by the fact that, as Mill astutely pointed out, unlike other oppressed groups or castes, men demand of them not only submission but unqualified affection as well; thus women are often weakened by the internalized demands of the male-dominated society itself, as well as by a plethora of material goods and comforts: the middle-class woman has a great deal more to lose than her chains.

The question "Why have there been no great women artists?" is simply the top tenth of an iceberg of misinterpretation and misconception; beneath lies a vast dark bulk of shaky *idées reçues* about the nature of art and its situational concomitants, about the nature of human abilities in general and of human excellence in particular, and the role that the social order plays in all of this. While the "woman problem" as such may be a pseudo-issue, the misconceptions involved in the question "Why have there been no great women artists?" points to major areas of intellectual obfuscation beyond the specific political and ideological issues involved in the subjection of women. Basic to the question are many naïve, distorted, uncritical assumptions about the making of art in general, as well as the making of great art. These assumptions, conscious or unconscious, link together such unlikely superstars as Michelangelo and van Gogh, Raphael and Jackson Pollock under the rubric of "Great"—an honorific attested to by the number of scholarly monographs devoted to the artist in question—and the Great Artist is, of course, conceived of as one who has "Genius"; Genius, in turn, is thought of as an atemporal and mysterious power somehow embedded in the person of the Great Artist.[6] Such ideas are related to unquestioned, often unconscious, meta-historical premises that make Hippolyte Taine's race-milieu-moment formulation of the dimensions of historical thought seem a model of sophistication. But these assumptions are intrinsic to a great deal of art-historical writing. It is no accident that the crucial question of the conditions *generally* productive of great art has so rarely been investigated, or that attempts to investigate such general problems have, until fairly recently, been dismissed as unscholarly, too broad, or the province of some other discipline, like sociology. To encourage a dispassionate, impersonal, sociological, and institutionally oriented approach would reveal the entire romantic, elitist, individual-glorifying, and monograph-producing substructure upon which the profession of art history is based, and which has only recently been called into question by a group of younger dissidents.

Underlying the question about woman as artist, then, we find the myth of the Great Artist—subject of a hundred monographs, unique, godlike—bearing within his person since birth a mysterious essence, rather like the golden nugget in Mrs. Grass's chicken soup, called Genius or Talent, which, like murder, must always out, no matter how unlikely or unpromising the circumstances.

The magical aura surrounding the representational arts and their creators has, of course, given birth to myths since the earliest times. Interestingly enough, the same magical abilities attributed by Pliny to the Greek sculptor Lysippos in antiquity—the mysterious

inner call in early youth, the lack of any teacher but Nature herself
—is repeated as late as the nineteenth century by Max Buchon in
his biography of Courbet. The supernatural powers of the artist as
imitator, his control of strong, possibly dangerous powers, have
functioned historically to set him off from others as a godlike creator, one who creates Being out of nothing. The fairy tale of the
discovery by an older artist or discerning patron of the Boy Wonder, usually in the guise of a lowly shepherd boy, has been a stock-in-
trade of artistic mythology ever since Vasari immortalized the
young Giotto, discovered by the great Cimabue while the lad was
guarding his flocks, drawing sheep on a stone; Cimabue, overcome
with admiration for the realism of the drawing, immediately invited
the humble youth to be his pupil.[7] Through some mysterious coinci-
dence, later artists including Beccafumi, Andrea Sansovino, Andrea
del Castagno, Mantegna, Zurbarán, and Goya were all discovered
in similar pastoral circumstances. Even when the young Great Artist was not fortunate enough to come equipped with a flock of sheep,
his talent always seems to have manifested itself very early, and
independent of any external encouragement: Filippo Lippi and
Poussin, Courbet and Monet are all reported to have drawn caricatures in the margins of their schoolbooks instead of studying the
required subjects—we never, of course, hear about the youths who
neglected their studies and scribbled in the margins of their notebooks without ever becoming anything more elevated than depart-
ment-store clerks or shoe salesmen. The great Michelangelo himself,
according to his biographer and pupil, Vasari, did more drawing
than studying as a child. So pronounced was his talent, reports
Vasari, that when his master, Ghirlandaio, absented himself momen-
tarily from his work in Santa Maria Novella, and the young art
student took the opportunity to draw "the scaffolding, trestles, pots
of paint, brushes and the apprentices at their tasks" in this brief
absence, he did it so skillfully that upon his return the master exclaimed: "This boy knows more than I do."

As is so often the case, such stories, which probably have some
truth in them, tend both to reflect and perpetuate the attitudes they
subsume. Even when based on fact, these myths about the early
manifestations of genius are misleading. It is no doubt true, for

example, that the young Picasso passed all the examinations for entrance to the Barcelona, and later to the Madrid, Academy of Art at the age of fifteen in but a single day, a feat of such difficulty that most candidates required a month of preparation. But one would like to find out more about similar precocious qualifiers for art academies who then went on to achieve nothing but mediocrity or failure—in whom, of course, art historians are uninterested—or to study in greater detail the role played by Picasso's art-professor father in the pictorial precocity of his son. What if Picasso had been born a girl? Would Señor Ruiz have paid as much attention or stimulated as much ambition for achievement in a little Pablita?

What is stressed in all these stories is the apparently miraculous, nondetermined, and asocial nature of artistic achievement; this semi-religious conception of the artist's role is elevated to hagiography in the nineteenth century, when art historians, critics, and, not least, some of the artists themselves tended to elevate the making of art into a substitute religion, the last bulwark of higher values in a materialistic world. The artist, in the nineteenth-century Saints' Legend, struggles against the most determined parental and social opposition, suffering the slings and arrows of social opprobrium like any Christian martyr, and ultimately succeeds against all odds—generally, alas, after his death—because from deep within himself radiates that mysterious, holy effulgence: Genius. Here we have the mad van Gogh, spinning out sunflowers despite epileptic seizures and near-starvation; Cézanne, braving paternal rejection and public scorn in order to revolutionize painting; Gauguin throwing away respectability and financial security with a single existential gesture to pursue his calling in the tropics; or Toulouse-Lautrec, dwarfed, crippled, and alcoholic, sacrificing his aristocratic birthright in favor of the squalid surroundings that provided him with inspiration.

Now no serious contemporary art historian takes such obvious fairy tales at their face value. Yet it is this sort of mythology about artistic achievement and its concomitants which forms the unconscious or unquestioned assumptions of scholars, no matter how many crumbs are thrown to social influences, ideas of the times, economic crises, and so on. Behind the most sophisticated investigations of great artists—more specifically, the art-historical monograph, which accepts the notion of the great artist as primary, and the social and institutional structures within which he lived and worked as mere secondary "influences" or "background"—lurks the golden-nugget theory of genius and the free-enterprise conception of individual achievement. On this basis, women's lack of major achievement in art may be formulated as a syllogism: If women had the golden nugget of artistic genius then it would reveal itself. But it has never revealed itself. Q.E.D. Women do not have the golden nugget of artistic genius. If Giotto, the obscure shepherd boy, and van Gogh with his fits could make it, why not women?

Yet as soon as one leaves behind the world of fairy tale and self-fulfilling prophecy and, instead, casts a dispassionate eye on the actual situations in which important art production has existed, in the total range of its social and institutional structures throughout history, one finds that the very questions which are fruitful or relevant for the historian to ask shape up rather differently. One would like to ask, for instance, from what social classes artists were most likely to come at different periods of art history, from what castes and subgroup. What proportion of painters and sculptors, or more specifically, of major painters and sculptors, came from families in which their fathers or other close relatives were painters and sculptors or engaged in related professions? As Nikolaus Pevsner points out in his discussion of the French Academy in the seventeenth and eighteenth centuries, the transmission of the artistic profession from father to son was considered a matter of course (as it was with the Coypels, the Coustous, the Van Loos, etc.); indeed, sons of academicians were exempted from the customary fees for lessons.[8] Despite the noteworthy and dramatically satisfying cases of the great father-rejecting *révoltés* of the nineteenth century, one might be forced to admit that a large proportion of artists, great and not-so-great, in the days when it was normal for sons to follow in their fathers' footsteps, had artist fathers. In the rank of major artists, the names of Holbein and Dürer, Raphael and Bernini, immediately spring to mind; even in our own times, one can cite the names of Picasso, Calder, Giacometti, and Wyeth as members of artist-families.

As far as the relationship of artistic occupation and social class is concerned, an interesting paradigm for the question "Why have there been no great women artists?" might well be provided by trying to answer the question "Why have there been no great artists from the aristocracy?" One can scarcely think, before the antitraditional nineteenth century at least, of any artist who sprang from the ranks of any more elevated class than the upper bourgeoisie; even in the nineteenth century, Degas came from the lower nobility—more like the haute bourgeoisie, in fact—and only Toulouse-Lautrec, metamorphosed into the ranks of the marginal by accidental deformity, could be said to have come from the loftier reaches of the upper classes. While the aristocracy has always provided the lion's share of the patronage and the audience for art—as, indeed, the aristocracy of wealth does even in our more democratic days—it has contributed little beyond amateurish efforts to the creation of art itself, despite the fact that aristocrats (like many women) have had more than their share of educational advantages, plenty of leisure and, indeed, like women, were often encouraged to dabble in the arts and even develop into respectable amateurs, like Napoleon III's cousin, the Princess Mathilde, who exhibited at the official Salons, or Queen Victoria, who, with Prince Albert, studied art with no less a figure than Landseer himself. Could it be that the little golden nugget—genius—is missing from the aristocratic makeup in the same way that it is from the feminine psyche? Or rather, is it not that the kinds of demands and expectations placed before both aristocrats and women—the amount of time necessarily devoted to social functions, the very kinds of activities demanded—simply made total devotion to professional art production out of the question, indeed unthinkable, both for upper-class males and for women generally, rather than its being a question of genius and talent?

When the right questions are asked about the conditions for producing art, of which the production of great art is a subtopic, there will no doubt have to be some discussion of the situational concomitants of intelligence and talent generally, not merely of artistic genius. Piaget and others have stressed in their genetic epistemology that in the development of reason and in the unfolding of imagination in young children, intelligence—or, by implication, what we choose to call genius—is a dynamic activity rather than a static essence, and an activity of a subject *in a situation*. As further investigations in the field of child development imply, these abilities, or this intelligence, are built up minutely, step by step, from infancy onward, and the patterns of adaptation-accommodation may be established so early within the subject-in-an-environment that they may indeed *appear* to be innate to the unsophisticated observer. Such investigations imply that, even aside from meta-historical reasons, scholars will have to abandon the notion, consciously articulated or not, of individual genius as innate, and as primary to the creation of art.[9]

The question "Why have there been no great women artists?" has led us to the conclusion, so far, that art is not a free, autonomous activity of a super-endowed individual, "influenced" by previous artists, and, more vaguely and superficially, by "social forces," but rather, that the total situation of art making, both in terms of the development of the art maker and in the nature and quality of the work of art itself, occur in a social situation, are integral elements of this social structure, and are mediated and determined by specific and definable social institutions, be they art academies, systems of patronage, mythologies of the divine creator, artist as he-man or social outcast.

The Question of the Nude

We can now approach our question from a more reasonable standpoint, since it seems probable that the answer to why there have been no great women artists lies not in the nature of individual genius or the lack of it, but in the nature of given social institutions and what they forbid or encourage in various classes or groups of individuals. Let us first examine such a simple, but critical, issue as availability of the nude model to aspiring women artists, in the period extending from the Renaissance until near the end of the nineteenth century, a period in which careful and prolonged study of the nude model was essential to the training of every young artist, to the production of any work with pretensions to grandeur, and to the very essence of History Painting, generally accepted as the highest category of art. Indeed, it was argued by defenders of traditional painting in the nineteenth century that there could be no great painting *with* clothed figures, since costume inevitably destroyed both the temporal universality and the classical idealization required by great art. Needless to say, central to the training programs of the academies since their inception late in the sixteenth and early in the seventeenth centuries, was life drawing from the nude, generally male, model. In addition, groups of artists and their pupils often met privately for life drawing sessions from the nude model in their studios. While individual artists and private academies employed the female model extensively, the female nude was forbidden in almost all public art schools as late as 1850 and after—a state of affairs which Pevsner rightly designates as "hardly believable."[10] Far more believable, unfortunately, was the complete unavailability to the aspiring woman artist of *any* nude models at all, male or female. As late as 1893, "lady" students were not admitted to life drawing at the Royal Academy in London, and even when they were, after that date, the model had to be "partially draped."[11]

A brief survey of representations of life-drawing sessions reveals: an all-male clientele drawing from the female nude in Rembrandt's studio; men working from male nudes in eighteenth-century representations of academic instruction in The Hague and Vienna; men working from the seated male nude in Boilly's charming painting of the interior of Houdon's studio at the beginning of the nineteenth century. Léon-Mathieu Cochereau's scrupulously veristic *Interior of David's Studio* [1], exhibited in the Salon of 1814, reveals a group of young men diligently drawing or painting from a male nude model, whose discarded shoes may be seen before the models' stand.

The very plethora of surviving "Academies"—detailed, painstaking studies from the nude studio model—in the youthful oeuvre of artists down through the time of Seurat and well into the twentieth century, attests to the central importance of this branch of study in the pedagogy and development of the talented beginner. The formal academic program itself normally proceeded, as a matter of course, from copying from drawings and engravings, to drawing from casts of famous works of sculpture, to drawing from the living model. To be deprived of this ultimate stage of training meant, in

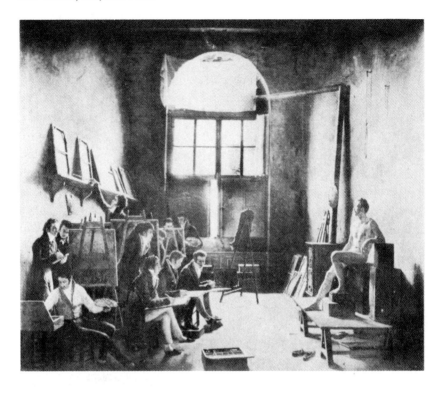

1. Léon-Mathieu Cochereau. *Interior of David's Studio*

effect, to be deprived of the possibility of creating major art works, unless one were a very ingenious lady indeed, or simply, as most of the women aspiring to be painters ultimately did, restricting oneself to the "minor" fields of portraiture, genre, landscape, or still life. It is rather as though a medical student were denied the opportunity to dissect or even examine the naked human body.

There exist, to my knowledge, no historical representations of artists drawing from the nude model which include women in any role but that of the nude model itself, an interesting commentary on rules of propriety: that is, it is all right for a ("low," of course) woman to reveal herself naked-as-an-object for a group of men, but forbidden to a woman to participate in the active study and record-ing of naked-man-as-an-object, or even of a fellow woman. An amusing example of this taboo on confronting a dressed lady with a naked man is embodied in a group portrait of the members of the Royal Academy in London in 1772, represented by Zoffany [2] as gathered in the life room before two nude male models: all the distinguished members are present with but one noteworthy exception—the single female member, the renowned Angelica Kauffmann, who, for propriety's sake, is merely present in effigy, in the form of a portrait hanging on the wall. A slightly earlier drawing, *Ladies in the Studio* by the Polish artist Daniel Chodowiecki, shows the ladies portraying a modestly dressed member of their sex. In a lithograph dating from the relatively liberated epoch following the French Revolution, the lithographer Marlet has represented some women sketchers in a group of students working from the male model, but the model himself has been chastely provided with what appears to be a pair of bathing trunks, a garment hardly conducive

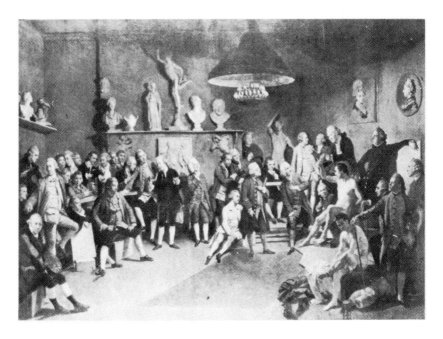

2. Johann Zoffany. *The Academicians of the Royal Academy*

to a sense of classical elevation; no doubt such license was considered daring in its day, and the young ladies in question suspected of doubtful morals, but even this liberated state of affairs seems to have lasted only a short while. In an English stereoscopic color view of the interior of a studio of about 1865, the standing, bearded male model is so heavily draped that not an iota of his anatomy escapes from the discreet toga, save for a single bare shoulder and arm: even so, he obviously had the grace to avert his eyes in the presence of the crinoline-clad young sketchers.

The women in the Women's Modeling Class at the Pennsylvania Academy were evidently not allowed even this modest privilege. A photograph by Thomas Eakins of about 1885 reveals these students modeling from a cow (bull? ox? the nether regions are obscure in the photograph), a naked cow to be sure, perhaps a daring liberty when one considers that even piano legs might be concealed beneath pantalettes during this era. (The idea of introducing a bovine model into the artist's studio stems from Courbet, who brought a bull into his short-lived studio academy in the 1860s). Only at the very end of the nineteenth century, in the relatively liberated and open atmosphere of Repin's studio and circle in Russia, do we find representations of women art students working uninhibitedly from the nude—the female model, to be sure—in the company of men. Even in this case, it must be noted that certain photographs represent a private sketch group meeting in one of the women artists' homes; in another, the model is draped; and the large group portrait, a cooperative effort by two men and two women students of Repin's, is an imaginary gathering together of all of the Russian realist's pupils, past and present, rather than a realistic studio view.

I have gone into the question of the availability of the nude model, a single aspect of the automatic, institutionally maintained discrimination against women, in such detail simply to demonstrate both the universality of this discrimination and its consequences, as well as the institutional rather than individual nature of but one facet of the necessary preparation for achieving mere proficiency, much less greatness, in the realm of art during a long period. One could equally well examine other dimensions of the situation, such as the apprenticeship system, the academic educational pattern which, in

France especially, was almost the only key to success and which had a regular progression and set competitions, crowned by the Prix de Rome which enabled the young winner to work in the French Academy in that city—unthinkable for women, of course—and for which women were unable to compete until the end of the nineteenth century, by which time, in fact, the whole academic system had lost its importance anyway. It seems clear, to take France in the nineteenth century as an example (a country which probably had a larger proportion of women artists than any other—that is to say, in terms of their percentage in the total number of artists exhibiting in the Salon), that "women were not accepted as professional painters."[12] In the middle of the century, there were only a third as many women as men artists, but even this mildly encouraging statistic is deceptive when we discover that out of this relatively meager number, *none* had attended that major stepping stone to artistic success, the École des Beaux-Arts, only 7 percent had received any official commission or had held any official office—and these might include the most menial sort of work—only 7 percent had ever received any Salon medal, and *none* had ever received the Legion of Honor.[13] Deprived of encouragements, educational facilities and rewards, it is almost incredible that a certain percentage of women did persevere and seek a profession in the arts.

It also becomes apparent why women were able to compete on far more equal terms with men—and even become innovators—in literature. While art making traditionally has demanded the learning of specific techniques and skills, in a certain sequence, in an institutional setting outside the home, as well as becoming familiar with a specific vocabulary of iconography and motifs, the same is by no means true for the poet or novelist. Anyone, even a woman, has to learn the language, can learn to read and write, and can commit personal experiences to paper in the privacy of one's room. Naturally this oversimplifies the real difficulties and complexities involved in creating good or great literature, whether by man or woman, but it still gives a clue as to the possibility of the existence of an Emily Brönte or an Emily Dickinson and the lack of their counterparts, at least until quite recently, in the visual arts.

Of course we have not gone into the "fringe" requirements for major artists, which would have been, for the most part, both psychically and socially closed to women, even if hypothetically they could have achieved the requisite grandeur in the performance of their craft: in the Renaissance and after, the great artist, aside from participating in the affairs of an academy, might well be intimate with members of humanist circles with whom he could exchange ideas, establish suitable relationships with patrons, travel widely and freely, perhaps politic and intrigue; nor have we mentioned the sheer organizational acumen and ability involved in running a major studio-factory, like that of Rubens. An enormous amount of self-confidence and worldly knowledgeability, as well as a natural sense of well-earned dominance and power, was needed by the great *chef d'école,* both in the running of the production end of painting, and in the control and instruction of the numerous students and assistants.

The Lady's Accomplishment

In contrast to the single-mindedness and commitment demanded of a *chef d'école,* we might set the image of the "lady painter" established by nineteenth-century etiquette books and reinforced by the literature of the times. It is precisely the insistence upon a modest, proficient, self-demeaning level of amateurism as a "suitable accomplishment" for the well-brought-up young woman, who naturally would want to direct her major attention to the welfare of others —family and husband—that militated, and still militates, against any real accomplishment on the part of women. It is this emphasis which transforms serious commitment to frivolous self-indulgence, busy work, or occupational therapy, and today, more than ever, in suburban bastions of the feminine mystique, tends to distort the whole notion of what art is and what kind of social role it plays. In Mrs. Ellis's widely read *The Family Monitor and Domestic Guide,* published before the middle of the nineteenth century, a book of advice popular both in the United States and in England, women were warned against the snare of trying too hard to excel in any one thing:

It must not be supposed that the writer is one who would advocate, as essential to woman, any very extraordinary degree of intellectual attainment, especially if confined to one particular branch of study. "I should like to excel in something" is a frequent and, to some extent, laudable expression; but in what does it originate, and to what does it tend? To be able to do a great many things tolerably well, is of infinitely more value to a woman, than to be able to excel in any one. By the former, she may render herself generally useful; by the latter, she may dazzle for an hour. By being apt, and tolerably well skilled in everything, she may fall into any situation in life with dignity and ease—by devoting her time to excellence in one, she may remain incapable of every other.

So far as cleverness, learning, and knowledge are conducive to woman's moral excellence, they are therefore desirable, and no further. All that would occupy her mind to the exclusion of better things, all that would involve her in the mazes of flattery and admiration, all that would tend to draw away her thoughts from others and fix them on herself, ought to be avoided as an evil to her, however brilliant or attractive it may be in itself.[14]

Lest we are tempted to laugh, we may refresh ourselves with more recent samples of exactly the same message cited in Betty Friedan's *Feminine Mystique,* or in the pages of recent issues of popular women's magazines.

The advice has a familiar ring: propped up by a bit of Freudianism and some tag-lines from the social sciences about the well-rounded personality, preparation for woman's chief career, marriage, and the unfemininity of deep involvement with work rather than sex, it is still the mainstay of the Feminine Mystique. Such an outlook helps guard men from unwanted competition in their "serious" professional activities and assures them of "well-rounded" assistance on the home front, so that they can have sex and family in addition to the fulfillment of their own specialized talents at the same time.

As far as painting specifically is concerned, Mrs. Ellis finds that it has one immediate advantage for the young lady over its rival branch of artistic activity, music—it is quiet and disturbs no one (this negative virtue, of course, would not be true of sculpture, but accomplishment with the hammer and chisel simply never occurs as a suitable accomplishment for the weaker sex); in addition, says Mrs. Ellis, "it [drawing] is an employment which beguiles the mind of many cares . . . Drawing is, of all other occupations, the one most calculated to keep the mind from brooding upon self, and to maintain that general cheerfulness which is a part of social and domestic duty . . . It can also," she adds, "be laid down and resumed, as circumstance or inclination may direct, and that without any serious loss."[15] Again, lest we feel that we have made a great deal of progress in this area in the past one hundred years, I might bring up the remark of a bright young doctor who, when the conversation turned to his wife and her friends "dabbling" in the arts, snorted: "Well, at least it keeps them out of trouble!" Now as in the nineteenth century, amateurism and lack of real commitment as well as snobbery and emphasis on chic on the part of women in their artistic "hobbies," feeds the contempt of the successful, professionally committed man who is engaged in "real" work and can, with a certain justice, point to his wife's lack of seriousness in her artistic activities. For such men, the "real" work of women is only that which directly or indirectly serves the family; any other commitment falls under the rubric of diversion, selfishness, egomania, or, at the unspoken extreme, castration. The circle is a vicious one, in which philistinism and frivolity mutually reenforce each other.

In literature, as in life, even if the woman's commitment to art was a serious one, she was expected to drop her career and give up this commitment at the behest of love and marriage: this lesson is, today as in the nineteenth century, still inculcated in young girls, directly or indirectly, from the moment they are born. Even the determined and successful heroine of Mrs. Craik's mid-nineteenth-century novel about feminine artistic success, *Olive*, a young woman who lives alone, strives for fame and independence, and actually supports herself through her art—such unfeminine behavior is at least partly excused by the fact that she is a cripple and automatically considers that marriage is denied to her—even Olive ultimately succumbs to the blandishments of love and marriage. To paraphrase the words of Patricia Thomson in *The Victorian Heroine*, Mrs. Craik, having shot her bolt in the course of her novel, is content, finally, to let her heroine, whose ultimate greatness the reader has never been able to doubt, sink gently into matrimony. "Of Olive, Mrs. Craik comments imperturbably that her husband's influence is to deprive the Scottish Academy of 'no one knew how many grand pictures.' "[16] Then as now, despite men's greater "tolerance," the choice for women seems always to be marriage *or* a career, i.e., solitude as the price of success *or* sex and companionship at the price of professional renunciation.

That achievement in the arts, as in any field of endeavor, demands struggle and sacrifice is undeniable; that this has certainly been true after the middle of the nineteenth century, when the traditional institutions of artistic support and patronage no longer fulfilled their customary obligations, is also undeniable. One has only to think of Delacroix, Courbet, Degas, van Gogh, and Toulouse-Lautrec as examples of great artists who gave up the distractions and obligations of family life, at least in part, so that they could pursue their artistic careers more singlemindedly. Yet none of them was automatically denied the pleasures of sex or companionship on account of this choice. Nor did they ever conceive that they had sacrificed their manhood or their sexual role on account of their singlemindedness in achieving professional fulfillment. But if the artist in question happened to be a woman, one thousand years of guilt, self-doubt, and objecthood would have been added to the undeniable difficulties of being an artist in the modern world.

The unconscious aura of titillation that arises from a visual representation of an aspiring woman artist in the mid-nineteenth century, Emily Mary Osborn's heartfelt painting, *Nameless and Friendless*, 1857 (see Figure 9, Chapter 1), a canvas representing a poor but lovely and respectable young girl at a London art dealer, nervously awaiting the verdict of the pompous proprietor about the worth of her canvases while two ogling "art lovers" look on, is really not too different in its underlying assumptions from an overtly salacious work like Bompard's *Debut of the Model* [3]. The theme in

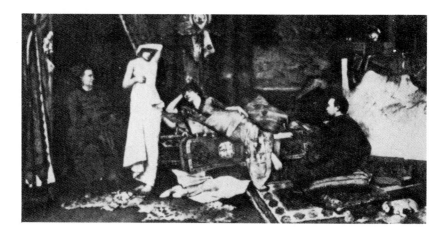

3. Maurice Bompard. *The Debut of the Model*

both is innocence, delicious feminine innocence, exposed to the world. It is the charming *vulnerability* of the young woman artist, like that of the hesitating model, which is really the subject of Osborn's painting, not the value of the young woman's work or her pride in it: the issue here is, as usual, sexual rather than serious. Always a model but never an artist might well have served as the motto of the seriously aspiring young woman in the arts of the nineteenth century.

Successes

But what of the small band of heroic women, who, throughout the ages, despite obstacles, have achieved preeminence, if not the pinnacles of grandeur of a Michelangelo, a Rembrandt, or a Picasso? Are there any qualities that may be said to have characterized them as a group and as individuals? While I cannot go into such an investigation in great detail in this article, I can point to a few striking characteristics of women artists generally: they all, almost without exception, were either the daughters of artist fathers, or, generally later, in the nineteenth and twentieth centuries, had a close personal connection with a stronger or more dominant male artistic personality. Neither of these characteristics is, of course, unusual for men artists, either, as we have indicated above in the case of artist fathers and sons: it is simply true almost *without exception* for their feminine counterparts, at least until quite recently. From the legendary sculptor, Sabina von Steinbach, in the thirteenth century, who, according to local tradition, was responsible for South Portal groups on the Cathedral of Strasbourg, down to Rosa Bonheur, the most renowned animal painter of the nineteenth century, and including such eminent women artists as Marietta Robusti, daughter of Tintoretto, Lavinia Fontana, Artemisia Gentileschi, Elizabeth Chéron, Mme Vigée-Lebrun, and Angelica Kauffmann—all, without exception, were the daughters of artists; in the nineteenth century, Berthe Morisot was closely associated with Manet, later marrying his brother, and Mary Cassatt based a good deal of her work on the style of her close friend Degas. Precisely the same breaking of traditional bonds and discarding of time-honored practices that permitted men artists to strike out in directions quite different from those of their fathers in the second half of the nineteenth century enabled women, with additional difficulties, to be sure, to strike out on their own as well. Many of our more recent women artists, like Suzanne Valadon, Paula Modersohn-Becker, Käthe Kollwitz, or Louise Nevelson, have come from nonartistic backgrounds, although many contemporary and near-contemporary women artists have married fellow artists.

It would be interesting to investigate the role of benign, if not outright encouraging, fathers in the formation of women professionals: both Käthe Kollwitz and Barbara Hepworth, for example, recall the influence of unusually sympathetic and supportive fathers on their artistic pursuits. In the absence of any thoroughgoing investigation, one can only gather impressionistic data about the presence or absence of rebellion against parental authority in women artists, and whether there may be more or less rebellion on the part of women artists than is true in the case of men or vice versa. One thing, however, is clear: for a woman to opt for a career at all, much less for a career in art, has required a certain amount of unconventionality, both in the past and at present; whether or not the woman artist rebels against or finds strength in the attitude of her family, she must in any case have a good strong streak of rebellion in her to make her way in the world of art at all, rather than submitting to the socially approved role of wife and mother, the only role to which every social institution consigns her automatically. It is only by adopting, however covertly, the "masculine" attributes of singlemindedness, concentration, tenaciousness, and absorption in ideas and craftsmanship for their own sake, that women have succeeded, and continue to succeed, in the world of art.

Rosa Bonheur

It is instructive to examine in greater detail one of the most successful and accomplished women painters of all time, Rosa Bonheur (1822–1899), whose work, despite the ravages wrought upon its estimation by changes of taste and a certain admitted lack of variety, still stands as an impressive achievement to anyone interested in the art of the nineteenth century and in the history of taste generally. Rosa Bonheur is a woman artist in whom, partly because of the magnitude of her reputation, all the various conflicts, all the internal and external contradictions and struggles typical of her sex and profession, stand out in sharp relief.

The success of Rosa Bonheur firmly establishes the role of institutions, and institutional change, as a necessary, if not a sufficient, cause of achievement in art. We might say that Bonheur picked a fortunate time to become an artist if she was, at the same time, to have the disadvantage of being a woman: she came into her own in the middle of the nineteenth century, a time in which the struggle between traditional history painting as opposed to the less pretentious and more freewheeling genre painting, landscape and still-life was won by the latter group hands down. A major change in the social and institutional support for art itself was well under way: with the rise of the bourgeoisie and the fall of the cultivated aristocracy, smaller paintings, generally of everyday subjects, rather than grandiose mythological or religious scenes were much in demand. To cite the Whites: "Three hundred provincial museums there might be, government commissions for public works there might be, but the only possible paid destinations for the rising flood of canvases were the homes of the bourgeoisie. History painting had not and never would rest comfortably in the middle-class parlor. 'Lesser' forms of image art—genre, landscape, still-life—did."[17] In mid-century France, as in seventeenth-century Holland, there was a tendency for artists to attempt to achieve some sort of security in a shaky market situation by specializing, by making a career out of a specific subject: animal painting was a very popular field, as the Whites point out, and Rosa Bonheur was no doubt its most accomplished and successful practitioner, followed in popularity only by the Barbizon painter Troyon (who at one time was so pressed for his paintings of cows that he hired another artist to brush in the backgrounds). Rosa Bonheur's rise to fame accompanied that of the Barbizon landscapists, supported by those canny dealers, the Durand-Ruels, who later moved on to the Impressionists. The Durand-Ruels were among the first dealers to tap the expanding market in movable decoration for the middle classes, to use the Whites' terminology. Rosa Bonheur's naturalism and ability to capture the individuality—even the "soul"—of each of her animal subjects coincided with bourgeois taste at the time. The same combination of qualities, with a much stronger dose of sentimentality and pathetic fallacy to be sure, likewise assured the success of her *animalier* contemporary, Landseer, in England.

Daughter of an impoverished drawing master, Rosa Bonheur quite naturally showed her interest in art early; at the same time, she exhibited an independence of spirit and liberty of manner which immediately earned her the label of tomboy. According to her own later accounts, her "masculine protest" established itself early; to what extent *any* show of persistence, stubbornness, and vigor would be counted as "masculine" in the first half of the nineteenth century is conjectural. Rosa Bonheur's attitude toward her father is somewhat ambiguous: while realizing that he had been influential in directing her towards her life's work, there is no doubt that she resented his thoughtless treatment of her beloved mother, and in her reminiscences, she half affectionately makes fun of his bizarre form of social idealism. Raimond Bonheur had been an active member of the short-lived Saint-Simonian community, established in the third decade of the nineteenth century by "Le Père" Enfantin at Menilmontant. Although in her later years Rosa Bonheur might have made fun of some of the more farfetched eccentricities of the members of the community, and disapproved of the additional strain which her father's apostolate placed on her overburdened mother, it is obvious that the Saint-Simonian ideal of equality for women— they disapproved of marriage, their trousered feminine costume was a token of emancipation, and their spiritual leader, Le Père Enfantin, made extraordinary efforts to find a Woman Messiah to share his reign—made a strong impression on her as a child, and may well have influenced her future course of behavior.

"Why shouldn't I be proud to be a woman?" she exclaimed to an interviewer. "My father, that enthusiastic apostle of humanity, many times reiterated to me that woman's mission was to elevate the human race, that she was the Messiah of future centuries. It is to his doctrines that I owe the great, noble ambition I have conceived for the sex which I proudly affirm to be mine, and whose independence I will support to my dying day. . . ."[18] When she was hardly more than a child, he instilled in her the ambition to surpass Mme Vigée-Lebrun, certainly the most eminent model she could be expected to follow, and he gave her early efforts every possible encouragement. At the same time, the spectacle of her uncomplaining mother's slow decline from sheer overwork and poverty might have been an even more realistic influence on her decision to control her own destiny and never to become the slave of a husband and children. What is particularly interesting from the modern feminist viewpoint is Rosa Bonheur's ability to combine the most vigorous and unapologetic masculine protest with unabashedly self-contradictory assertions of "basic" femininity.

In those refreshingly straightforward pre-Freudian days, Rosa Bonheur could explain to her biographer that she had never wanted to marry for fear of losing her independence. Too many young girls let themselves be led to the altar like lambs to the sacrifice, she maintained. Yet at the same time that she rejected marriage for herself and implied an inevitable loss of selfhood for any woman who engaged in it, she, unlike the Saint-Simonians, considered marriage "a sacrament indispensable to the organization of society."

While remaining cool to offers of marriage, she joined in a

seemingly cloudless, lifelong, and apparently Platonic union with a fellow woman artist, Nathalie Micas, who evidently provided her with the companionship and emotional warmth which she needed. Obviously the presence of this sympathetic friend did not seem to demand the same sacrifice of genuine commitment to her profession which marriage would have entailed: in any case, the advantages of such an arrangement for women who wished to avoid the distraction of children in the days before reliable contraception are obvious.

Yet at the same time that she frankly rejected the conventional feminine role of her times, Rosa Bonheur still was drawn into what Betty Friedan has called the "frilly blouse syndrome," that innocuous version of the feminine protest which even today compels successful women psychiatrists or professors to adopt some ultra-feminine item of clothing or insist on proving their prowess as pie-bakers.[19] Despite the fact that she had early cropped her hair and adopted men's clothes as her habitual attire, following the example of George Sand, whose rural Romanticism exerted a powerful influence over her imagination, to her biographer she insisted, and no doubt sincerely believed, that she did so only because of the specific demands of her profession. Indignantly denying rumors to the effect that she had run about the streets of Paris dressed as a boy in her youth, she proudly provided her biographer with a daguerreotype of herself at sixteen, dressed in perfectly conventional feminine fashion, except for her shorn head, which she excused as a practical measure taken after the death of her mother; "Who would have taken care of my curls?" she demanded.[20]

As far as the question of masculine dress was concerned, she was quick to reject her interlocutor's suggestion that her trousers were a symbol of emancipation. "I strongly blame women who renounce their customary attire in the desire to make themselves pass for men," she affirmed. "If I had found that trousers suited my sex, I would have completely gotten rid of my skirts, but this is not the case, nor have I ever advised my sisters of the palette to wear men's clothes in the ordinary course of life. If, then, you see me dressed as I am, it is not at all with the aim of making myself interesting, as all too many women have tried, but simply in order to facilitate my work. Remember that at a certain period I spent whole days in the slaughterhouses. Indeed, you have to love your art in order to live in pools of blood . . . I was also fascinated with horses, and where better can one study these animals than at the fairs . . . ? I had no alternative but to realize that the garments of my own sex were a total nuisance. That is why I decided to ask the Prefect of Police for the authorization to wear masculine clothing.[21] But the costume I am wearing is my working outfit, nothing else. The remarks of fools have never bothered me. Nathalie [her companion] makes fun of them as I do. It doesn't bother her at all to see me dressed as a man, but if you are even the slightest bit put off, I am completely prepared to put on a skirt, especially since all I have to do is to open a closet to find a whole assortment of feminine outfits."[22]

At the same time Rosa Bonheur was forced to admit: "My trousers have been my great protectors. . . . Many times I have congratulated myself for having dared to break with traditions which would have forced me to abstain from certain kinds of work, due to the obligation to drag my skirts everywhere. . . ." Yet the famous artist again felt obliged to qualify her honest admission with an ill-assumed "femininity": "Despite my metamorphoses of costume, there is not a daughter of Eve who appreciates the niceties more than I do; my brusque and even slightly unsociable nature has never prevented my heart from remaining completely feminine."[23]

It is somewhat pathetic that this highly successful artist, unsparing of herself in the painstaking study of animal anatomy, diligently pursuing her bovine or equine subjects in the most unpleasant surroundings, industriously producing popular canvases throughout the course of a lengthy career, firm, assured, and incontrovertibly masculine in her style, winner of a first medal in the Paris Salon, Officer of the Legion of Honor, Commander of the Order of Isabella the Catholic and the Order of Leopold of Belgium, friend of Queen Victoria—that this world-renowned artist should feel compelled late in life to justify and qualify her perfectly reasonable assumption of masculine ways, for any reason whatsoever, and to feel compelled to attack her less modest trouser-wearing sisters at the same time, in order to satisfy the demands of her own conscience. For her conscience, despite her supportive father, her unconventional behavior, and the accolade of worldly success, still condemned her for not being a "feminine" woman.

The difficulties imposed by such demands on the woman artist continue to add to her already difficult enterprise even today. Compare, for example, the noted contemporary, Louise Nevelson, with her combination of utter, "unfeminine" dedication to her work and her conspicuously "feminine" false eyelashes; her admission that she got married at seventeen despite her certainty that she couldn't live without creating because "the world said you should get married."[24] Even in the case of these two outstanding artists—and whether we like *The Horse Fair* [4] or not, we still must admire Rosa Bonheur's professional achievement—the voice of the feminine mystique with its potpourri of ambivalent narcissism and guilt, internalized, subtly dilutes and subverts that total inner confidence, that absolute certitude and self-determination, moral and esthetic, demanded by the highest and most innovative work in art.

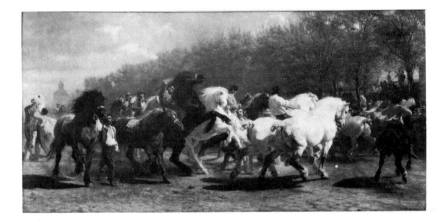

4. Rosa Bonheur. *The Horse Fair*

Conclusion

I have tried to deal with one of the perennial questions used to challenge women's demand for true, rather than token, equality, by examining the whole erroneous intellectual substructure upon which the question "Why have there been no great women artists?" is based; by questioning the validity of the formulation of so-called problems in general and the "problem" of women specifically; and then, by probing some of the limitations of the discipline of art history itself. By stressing the *institutional*—that is, the public—rather than the *individual*, or private, preconditions for achievement or the lack of it in the arts, I have tried to provide a paradigm for the investigation of other areas in the field. By examining in some detail a single instance of deprivation or disadvantage—the unavailability of nude models to women art students—I have suggested that it was indeed *institutionally* made impossible for women to achieve artistic excellence, or success, on the same footing as men, *no matter what* the potency of their so-called talent, or genius. The existence of a tiny band of successful, if not great, women artists throughout history does nothing to gainsay this fact, any more than does the existence of a few superstars or token achievers among the members of any minority groups. And while great achievement is rare and difficult at best, it is still rarer and more difficult if, while you work, you must at the same time wrestle with inner demons of self-doubt and guilt and outer monsters of ridicule or patronizing encouragement, neither of which have any specific connection with the quality of the art work as such.

What is important is that women face up to the reality of their history and of their present situation, without making excuses or puffing mediocrity. Disadvantage may indeed be an excuse; it is not, however, an intellectual position. Rather, using as a vantage point their situation as underdogs in the realm of grandeur, and outsiders in that of ideology, women can reveal institutional and intellectual weaknesses in general, and, at the same time that they destroy false consciousness, take part in the creation of institutions in which clear thought—and true greatness—are challenges open to anyone, man or woman, courageous enough to take the necessary risk, the leap into the unknown.

Notes

1. Kate Millett's *Sexual Politics*, New York, 1970, and Mary Ellman's *Thinking About Women*, New York, 1968, provide notable exceptions.

2. "Women Artists." Review of *Die Frauen in die Kunstgeschichte* by Ernst Guhl in *The Westminster Review* (American Edition), LXX, July 1858, pp. 91–104. I am grateful to Elaine Showalter for having brought this review to my attention.

3. See, for example, Peter S. Walch's excellent studies of Angelica Kauffmann or his unpublished doctoral dissertation, "Angelica Kauffmann," Princeton University, 1968, on the subject; for Artemisia Gentileschi, see R. Ward Bissell, "Artemisia Gentileschi—A New Documented Chronology," *Art Bulletin*, L (June 1968): 153–68.

4. New York, 1968.

5. John Stuart Mill, *The Subjection of Women* (1869) in *Three Essays by John Stuart Mill*, World's Classics Series, London, 1966, p. 441.

6. For the relatively recent genesis of the emphasis on the artist as the nexus of esthetic experience, see M. H. Abrams, *The Mirror and the Lamp: Romantic Theory and the Critical Tradition*, New York, 1953, and Maurice Z. Shroder, *Icarus: The Image of the Artist in French Romanticism*, Cambridge, Massachusetts, 1961.

7. A comparison with the parallel myth for women, the Cinderella story, is revealing: Cinderella gains higher status on the basis of a passive, "sex-object" attribute—small feet—whereas the Boy Wonder always proves himself through active accomplishment. For a thorough study of myths about artists, see Ernst Kris and Otto Kurz. *Die Legende vom Künstler: Ein Geschichtlicher Versuch*, Vienna, 1934.

8. Nikolaus Pevsner, *Academies of Art, Past and Present.* Cambridge, 1940, p. 96f.

9. Contemporary directions—earthworks, conceptual art, art as information, etc.— certainly point *away* from emphasis on the individual genius and his salable products; in art history, Harrison C. and Cynthia A. White's *Canvases and Careers: Institutional Change in the French Painting World*, New York, 1965, opens up a fruitful new direction of investigation, as did Nikolaus Pevsner's pioneering *Academies of Art*. Ernst Gombrich and Pierre Francastel, in their very different ways, always have tended to view art and the artist as part of a total situation rather than in lofty isolation.

10. Female models were introduced in the life class in Berlin in 1875, in Stockholm in 1839, in Naples in 1870, at the Royal College of Art in London after 1875. Pevsner, op. cit., p. 231. Female models at the Pennsylvania Academy of the Fine Arts wore masks to hide their identity as late as about 1866—as attested to in a charcoal drawing by Thomas Eakins—if not later.

11. Pevsner, op. cit., p. 231.

12. H. C. and C. A. White, op. cit., p. 51.

13. Ibid., Table 5.

14. Mrs. Ellis, *The Daughters of England: Their Position in Society, Character, and Responsibilities* (1844) in *The Family Monitor*, New York, 1844, p. 35.

15. Ibid., pp. 38–39.

16. Patricia Thomson, *The Victorian Heroine: A Changing Ideal*, London, 1956, p. 77.

17. H. C. and C. A. White, op. cit., p. 91.

18. Anna Klumpke, *Rosa Bonheur: Sa Vie, son oeuvre,* Paris, 1908, p. 311.

19. Betty Friedan, *The Feminine Mystique,* New York, 1963, p. 158.

20. A. Klumpke, op. cit., p. 166.

21. Paris, like many cities even today, had laws against cross-dressing on its books.

22. A. Klumpke, op. cit., pp. 308-9.

23. Ibid., pp. 310-11.

24. Cited in Elizabeth Fisher, "The Woman as Artist, Louise Nevelson," *Aphra* I (Spring 1970): 32.

Index of Artists

Page numbers in *italics* refer to illustrations.

Linda Nochlin was born in Brooklyn, New York, where she attended the Ethical Culture School and Midwood High School. She graduated from Vassar College in 1951 with a degree in philosophy, got her masters degree in seventeenth-century English literature from Columbia University in 1952, and then was invited back to teach art history at Vassar in 1952; she went on to get her doctorate in art history at the Institute of Fine Arts of New York University. Her doctoral dissertation was on Gustave Courbet, a subject which has continued to interest her over the years: she is co-curator of the exhibition "Courbet Reconsidered," which opened at the Brooklyn Museum in November 1988. Her special area of interest is in the art of the nineteenth century, and she has published widely in the field, including such works as *Realism* (nominated for the National Book Award) and many articles on such artists as Courbet, Manet, and Degas.

Her published work in feminist art history started in 1971 with the article "Why Have There Been No Great Women Artists?," generally considered to be the first work in the field, and has continued down to the present day. *Women, Art, and Power* brings together the work of almost twenty years of scholarship and speculation. In addition to writing, Professor Nochlin was Mary Conover Mellon Professor at Vassar College for many years, has taught at Columbia, Stanford, Williams, and Hunter College, and is at present Distinguished Professor of Art History at the Graduate Center of the City University of New York. She has lectured widely in major colleges, universities, and museums in this country and in France. She is married to architectural historian Richard Pommer and has two daughters, Jessica Nochlin Trotta and Daisy Pommer, and a granddaughter.

J Elliott, July '94